P9-CRH-734

Praise for *The High-Speed Company*

"Defines the fundamentals that separate successful organizations from also-rans. This book should be required reading for all CEOs and board members."
— Glenn A. Fosdick, CEO (2001–2013), The Nebraska Medical Center, one of the world's preeminent medical facilities

"No matter the industry, Jason Jennings reveals through his research and inspirational stories what we all knew in our hearts: Speed is driven by purpose. We are all wired to work on something bigger than ourselves, Jennings takes us down the path to get there."
— Richard Sheridan, CEO and chief storyteller, Menlo Innovations; author of *Joy, Inc.*

"Jennings provides real-world examples of how the most successful organizations have developed a culture of urgency. A must read for any business leader." — Tiffani Bova, vice president, distinguished analyst, Gartner

Praise for *The Reinventors*

"*The Reinventors* should find a home on many executives' desks, as the time is now to begin the process of serially reinventing your business, to highlight companies that are good at it, and to teach other leaders how to master the skill. . . . [Jennings] will teach you how to figure it out for yourself, how to be more aggressively innovative, how to become a serial reinventor."
— Jack Covert, 800-CEO-READ

"Leadership and management expert Jennings (*Hit the Ground Running*) believes that companies have to continually change and adapt to their environment. . . . With analyses of such companies as Southwest Airlines and Apple, Jennings offers engaging business stories and perhaps a nugget of wisdom for corporate managers." — *Publishers Weekly*

"*The Reinventors* rocks! Jennings has done it again and delivers a crisp step-by-step set of instructions for embracing constant radical change and achieving nonstop growth. If you're ready, this is your blueprint for success."
— Guy Kawasaki, bestselling author of *Enchantment, Reality Check,* and *The Art of the Start*

"*The Reinventors* is an extremely timely, practical, and interesting book. Everyone needs to be able to reinvent and constantly change, yet we aren't taught how. This book will show you the way."
— Peter Sims, bestselling author of *Little Bets*

"This is a fast-paced, well-written book on the overriding importance of change, innovation, evolution, and maybe even revolution as key requirements for long-term success in any organization. Turmoil is good; comfortable stasis is fatal. Jennings nails it."

—Bob Lutz, former vice chairman, General Motors;
bestselling author of *Car Guys vs. Bean Counters*

"Open this book to any page and you'll learn something: It's a fascinating, accessible, and practical way of rethinking your company and gaining edge in today's hypercompetitive marketplace. Plus, it's a blast to read. The guy can write and he clearly cares about helping you achieve greater success."

—Stan Slap, *New York Times* bestselling author of
Bury My Heart at Conference Room B

"Jennings is clearly becoming *the* successor to Peter Drucker. Once again, he's done a masterful job of researching the world for proven insights on how to reinvent a business and drive sustainable, profitable growth. His ideas are simultaneously practical, unexpected, and powerful. Use them every day to succeed."

—Dan Coughlin, consultant; author of *Beat Yesterday* and *The Management 500*

"If you're uncomfortable with the thought of becoming obsolete, read this book! *The Reinventors* delivers novel ways to pivot, spin, and solve your way into the future. This is classic Jason Jennings."

—Tim Sanders, founder of Net Minds; *New York Times*
bestselling author of *Love Is the Killer App*

THE
HIGH-SPEED
COMPANY

ALSO BY JASON JENNINGS

The Reinventors
Hit the Ground Running
Think Big, Act Small
Less is More

THE
HIGH-SPEED
COMPANY

CREATING URGENCY AND GROWTH
IN A NANOSECOND CULTURE

JASON
JENNINGS

with LAURENCE HAUGHTON

Portfolio / Penguin

PORTFOLIO / PENGUIN
Published by the Penguin Group
Penguin Group (USA) LLC
375 Hudson Street
New York, New York 10014

(penguin logo)

USA | Canada | UK | Ireland | Australia | New Zealand | India | South Africa | China
penguin.com
A Penguin Random House Company

First published by Portfolio / Penguin, a member of Penguin Group (USA) LLC, 2015

Copyright © 2015 by Jason Jennings
Penguin supports copyright. Copyright fuels creativity, encourages diverse voices,
promotes free speech, and creates a vibrant culture. Thank you for buying an authorized
edition of this book and for complying with copyright laws by not reproducing, scanning,
or distributing any part of it in any form without permission. You are supporting writers
and allowing Penguin to continue to publish books for every reader.

Grateful acknowledgment is made for permission to reprint an excerpt from
Bluebeard: A Novel by Kurt Vonnegut. Copyright © 1987 by Kurt Vonnegut.
Used by permission of Dell Publishing, an imprint of Random House,
a division of Random House LLC. All rights reserved.

ISBN 978-1-59184-736-6

Printed in the United States of America
1   3   5   7   9   10   8   6   4   2

Set in Adobe Caslon
Designed by Spring Hoteling

To Myron P. Patten, founder, former CEO, and chairman of The Patten Company. Very early in my career he took the time to listen to me and lead and encourage me in the pursuit of my goals, ambitions, and dreams.

He was a remarkable mentor.

CONTENTS

THE
HIGH-SPEED
COMPANY

Introduction: Urgency and Growth

"We need to create a greater sense of urgency and get things done faster."

Over the past dozen years, I've interviewed over eleven thousand CEOs, business owners, and highly successful entrepreneurs about their businesses and how they lead companies through good times and bad. One of the most important questions I ask them is "What's the biggest worry keeping you awake at night?"

The response is practically unanimous: Leaders worry about creating a sense of urgency in their organizations and operating quickly in an increasingly complex world. They want to create strong teams that are primed to handle any hurdle that comes their way and "get things done faster."

To understand why creating a high-speed company is most leaders' biggest challenge—and best way to ensure business success—all you need to do is recall the story of two huge companies: Sears and Kmart. Do you remember the glory days of Sears and Kmart between the sixties and 2000? Sears was "where America shops," the number one retailer, followed by a surging Kmart in second place. Walmart was a distant third, not considered worthy of serious attention. I can just imagine the insiders from Chicago scoffing, "Those people are from Arkansas, for crying out loud."

Watching those two retail giants over the past decade, however, has been like witnessing a train wreck in slow motion. Walmart surpassed Kmart and then Sears. Years of missteps spurred Sears and Kmart to merge into one company, where they completely lost their culture and urgency. Both their number of locations and their combined revenues have withered ten years in a row. As Sears and Kmart executives gather for their daily meeting with CEO Edward Lampert, they are plagued by doubts. "You never know what the plan or strategy is," one anonymous executive shared in *Crain's Chicago Business*. "What are we building? What are the criteria for success?" These once-lauded companies have taken big tumbles, thanks in no small part to operating as low-speed companies in an increasingly fast and complex world.

Meanwhile, Walmart has worked relentlessly to perfect a culture of urgency and growth using many of the strategies detailed in these pages. As of this writing, it's grown to more than ten thousand locations worldwide and, with a half trillion dollars in annual sales, its revenues are fifteen times those of Sears and Kmart combined. Truly a high-speed company positioned to succeed.

Similarly, look to the trajectories of BlackBerry and Apple—another prime example of how only cultures of growth and urgency survive. Just a few years ago, it was hard to find anyone in business who didn't have a BlackBerry. But the company, flush with a huge stash of cash, kept repeatedly delaying the release of the Black-Berry 10, confident its customers would wait and arrogantly stating the device's release would happen when the *company* was ready. The marketplace refused to wait, and Apple and Samsung swooped in to change the way the world communicates, selling billions of devices within a few years. J. K. Shin of Samsung and Steve Jobs and Tim Cook of Apple keenly understood the need for urgency and led their companies to become two of the world's most valuable in record-setting time.

The number one priority for business leaders today is creating organizations that work with a fierce sense of urgency in our crazy-busy world and keep their eye firmly fixed on growth. All of my conversations with CEOs and executives identify that pain point—and what I've found, and will share in this book, are tactics for building the fastest, most adaptive, strongest organizations that are set up to succeed in this nanosecond environment.

STAY IN THE FAST LANE

In 2014 the consulting firm McKinsey published a report titled "Grow Fast or Die Slow," an analysis of the fates and fortunes of three thousand software and Internet-services companies. The study concludes that companies that combine urgency and growth (groups growing 60 percent or more a year) deliver five times the returns to shareholders and are eight times more likely to reach $1 billion in revenues. The report also confirms that companies that don't maintain that culture or that take their foot off the pedal have only a one in three chance of ever getting back in the fast lane. Even in the more forgiving sectors outside of high technology, a lack of urgency and growth is a death knell for organizations. Less than one in two companies get back on the growth highway at all after they stall. Most are acquired, downsize, or go bankrupt.

Some people think that high-speed companies—those that have created a sense of urgency about getting to where they want to go—must be full of type A executives who force their staffs to tolerate incredible stress and be hasty, impulsive, and frantic. Nothing is further from the truth!

High-speed companies actually breathe easier, burn less energy, are never frantic, and get to the destinations they've chosen before the competition. Most have a lot of fun along the way. The key to their cultures of urgency and growth is that their leaders have figured out that speed is the thrill, exhilaration, and pride that comes with getting rid of the misguided things that most companies do that end up slowing them down and getting them stuck.

Real cultures of speed and urgency are able to do the following:

- Solve problems the first time rather than revisiting them again and again
- Keep good customers from defecting
- Empower the 70 percent of all employees who say they're not engaged or actively disengaged (per Gallup's "State of the American Workplace Report 2013") to start doing their part for the organization
- Allow people to admit mistakes rather than covering them up
- Encourage people to improvise rather than wait for direction from the top
- Reduce resistance to new ideas
- Get more cooperation and coordination across functions and titles
- Fill open jobs with people who like being fast
- Do all of the preceding simultaneously

It's not easy to set up a culture ready to execute at this level. It requires stretching your organizational muscles in a way you might not be used to—but it's the only way to set your company up for success today. And the more deeply you integrate these high-speed practices into your company, the better prepared you will be for whatever lies ahead. After all, who do you think is more out of breath, exasperated, and frantic: the fast folks at Samsung, Apple, and Walmart looking ahead to the next big thing in their industry or the people at BlackBerry, Sears, and Kmart worried about their jobs and the relevance of what their companies do?

BE FAST OR DIE SLOW

The digital revolution that's just beginning will continue to disrupt and wreak havoc on the traditional ways that *all* businesses have been led and managed. Eventually everything becomes a commodity and the marketplace sets the price. But now *eventually* takes days or months instead of years. Further, relationships don't count as they once did. "It's all about relationships and getting people to like you" was the advice given by the old-timers to newbies, and it worked well for decades. The global economic meltdown of 2008–9 and the subsequent microscopic scrutiny of every expense mean that no one can justify doing business with someone *just* because they're friends. To top it off, unless you're able to provide skilled workers a future filled with more challenging work, professional growth, and the rewards that go along with it, they'll leave and either join your competition or become your new competitors.

Unless a company—including yours—is changing faster on the inside than the world is changing on the outside, there's only grief on the horizon.

And know this: Being fast doesn't mean announcing you're going to change the world and then quickly renting offices, hiring a band of cool people, and generating mammoth buzz in social media. Being fast and building a culture of urgency and growth means finding, keeping, and growing the right workers and customers and consistently bringing in enough revenue to reward the people and the investors who made an investment of their time or money in the idea. It means proving you can meet your goals over and over again and showing the marketplace that you're not a one-trick pony.

OUR RESEARCH

These lessons about what makes a high-speed company aren't pulled out of thin air—they have been culled over decades of research into hundreds of thousands of companies worldwide.

Laurence Haughton,* my director of research and development, and I, aided by research teams of MBA students and various outside research firms like FactSet and Information On Demand, have evaluated the financial performance of 220,000 businesses, including every publicly traded company in the world, as well as the largest privately held companies in the world.†

Once a company's financial performance marks it as worthy of further study (and we've identified more than fifty thousand whose do) we begin gathering information about its structure, performance, longevity, leadership, and more. We build files and look for vulnerabilities that would disqualify it from inclusion in further research. Reasons for disqualification include being unable to verify financial performance; sudden and significant drops in revenue,

---

*Throughout the book "I" refers to me—Jason Jennings—and "we" refers to Laurence Haughton and me, working, researching, thinking, and writing in collaboration. Professionally we share one voice.

†You might expect a book about high-speed organizations to include many examples of brand-new tech companies that are redefining fast business. But that's not the case. Over the years, I've seen plenty of business books make big claims about companies that were old news or even extinct within weeks of the books' releases—done in by scandal, the end of a bubble, or other reasons. I have never and will never write about a company that hasn't been around long enough to prove its staying power.

profits, or market share; the departure of the leadership team that led the company to greatness; and credible accusations or lawsuits that call the firm's ethics into question.

Next we try to gain access to the company's CEO in order to conduct in-depth interviews. This sounds easier than it is. Getting inside these companies is the hardest part of our process; many companies and leaders are very protective of their processes and success. But we're dogged and determined to find out what makes these winners work, so we cajole, call in favors, ask nicely over and over again, and appeal to people's sense of fair play. Eventually we get inside these companies (only two have ever shut us out and they went on to fail, which probably means they'd seen the handwriting on the wall and that was why they didn't give us access) and dig in deep to see how they really tick—and bring you those findings in our book. These pages are the distillation of everything my teams and I have learned about how great companies build cultures based on urgency and growth.

OUR PROMISE

My intention is that any business owner, senior executive, CEO, or entrepreneur be able to read this book and put its contents into practice to build and sustain his or her own high-speed company. Middle managers, without the ability to implement significant change in their organizations, will benefit greatly as well because these findings will prepare them to lead and build cultures of urgency and growth when the opportunity arises.

If you're ready to get to work and transform your business, I suggest you read the book from start to finish and do the fast tasks found at the end of each chapter before moving on to the next. Following the chapters this way and implementing the takeaways will ensure that you end up with a durable culture that thinks fast and moves faster.

That said, not all people necessarily start at the beginning of a book and read to the end. If you're faced with a particular business problem, you might prefer to review the table of contents and go directly to the chapter that addresses what's on your mind at that moment. We've arranged the book so that you can use the chapters as a series of applications as well: Find the one that speaks most to what you're dealing with right now—such as drilling down on your values, transparency, or stewardship—and get to work applying those takeaways to your organization.

Because I travel between two hundred thousand and three hundred thousand miles each year, I've watched thousands of people read books on airplanes, so this book is also designed as an airplane read. Open any page and you will find something: an inspiration, an insight, or an instruction for going from great idea to fast and flawless execution. This little book is filled with big stories and ideas, even bigger lessons, and a bunch of business heroes who will help you build your high-speed company.

If you put the principles contained in the following pages to work, you will end up with a culture of urgency and growth and be able to succeed in a nanosecond world.

My greatest personal happiness is helping principled people achieve their full economic potential. I hope this book becomes your trusted coach and cheering section all rolled into one. That's the spirit in which it was researched and written for you.

Jason Jennings
Tiburon, California &
Timber Rock Shore,
Michigamme, Michigan
2014

CHAPTER ONE
Purpose

This is the true joy in life, being used for a purpose recognized by yourself as a mighty one. Being a force of nature instead of a feverish, selfish little clod of ailments and grievances, complaining that the world will not devote itself to making you happy.

—George Bernard Shaw

DOING WELL BY DOING GOOD

"How did you do on the quiz, Mr. Jennings?" asked my always prim-and-proper high school Latin teacher, Mrs. Anderson.

"Good," I mumbled, though I probably hadn't. I'd been too busy playing basketball the night before to study.

Mrs. Anderson scrunched her forehead and shook her finger. "Incorrect, Mr. Jennings. Superman does *good*. You did *well*."

Fast-forward a few years to my first year of college. I was sitting in Economics 101 and Nobel Prize winner Milton Friedman was on the screen, scrunching his forehead and shaking his finger just like Mrs. Anderson.

"There is one and *only* one responsibility of business," he declared, "and that's to make as much money as possible." He was dismissing those who were promoting the then-new idea that a business had a social responsibility to do good. Business needs to do well, according to Friedman—not do good.

Believing that great leaders must focus on making as much profit as possible, do this any way they're able, and leave it to others to do good works creates a major obstacle for any business that wants to become a high-speed company.

Companies with a proven record of urgency and growth—from the smallest to the largest—have torn down that figurative wall between doing well and doing good. They know that creating a strong sense of purpose, tied into doing something good, gets people off the fence and into taking urgent action. These purposes are not the long, boring, unmemorable vision and mission statements of previous decades. Those "visioning statements" flopped, failing to arouse anyone (other than maybe the person or committee who wrote them), igniting no urgency or growth. Truly fast companies can tell you what they do and why they do it—and get you excited about it—in only a few words.

Groundbreaking research by neuroscientists that tests how our brain's chemistry guides action (such as that by Dr. Matthew D. Lieberman, professor of psychiatry and biobehavioral sciences at UCLA and author of *Social: Why Our Brains Are Wired to Connect*) concludes that we are motivated by a greater good to try harder, work faster, persevere longer, cooperate better, and control our least productive impulses. And it's not just our productivity; other studies, including research by Dr. Victor Strecher of the University of Michigan, Barbara Fredrickson of UNC Chapel Hill, and Steve Cole of UCLA, demonstrate that meaning from a shared good purpose also helps reduce stress and improves health. Doing good can and does buy happiness. Imagine what a company can accomplish if hundreds or thousands of people are united by a shared purpose.

Four Words That Made a High-Speed Company

One high-speed company that's built a culture of urgency and growth is, perhaps surprisingly, a bank—a big bank, one of those supposedly dark forces of evil that almost caused the world's financial system to crash. But Denver-based CoBank is the opposite of what we've heard about most banks and bankers. In fact, CoBank is so unlike conventional financial organizations that CEO Bob Engel's playbook and the bank's accomplishments may be hard to believe.

CoBank is a nondepository, cooperative bank (like a credit union, it is owned by its customers) whose customers are agribusinesses; rural power, water, and communication providers; and other farm credit associations that serve more than seventy thousand farmers and ranchers. As a member of the U.S. Farm Credit System, Co-Bank supports the borrowing needs of agriculture and the nation's rural economy and does business in all fifty U.S. states.

With $100 billion in assets, CoBank ranks right up there alongside familiar banking names like Morgan Stanley, Union Bank, and Goldman Sachs. The big difference between them is earnings. Morgan Stanley generates a profit of about $65,000 annually for each of its 55,000 employees; Union Bank earns $63,000 for each of its 10,000 workers; and Goldman Sachs earns $235,394 for each of the 32,000 members of its workforce. By contrast, CoBank makes a profit of $1 million per employee per year, almost half of which is returned to its member owners. Other banks with comparable assets average 12,000 employees each—arguably meaning that CoBank's 850 workers are twelve times more productive than those of the other big banks. According to *Global Finance* magazine, CoBank is the single safest bank in the nation. Further, unlike many other banks, CoBank's financial performance was not affected by the financial crisis. In fact, in 2013 it finished its fourteenth consecutive year of increased earnings. In little more than a decade, it has grown its assets by 300 percent and profits by 600 percent. CoBank has proven that with a culture of urgency and growth it's possible to maintain velocity for years.

So how does CoBank do it? How has it mobilized its organization to consistently hit great numbers and preserve a stellar reputation in a damaged industry during the toughest times banking has ever faced? In speaking with Bob Engel, I learned that CoBank's success is directly attributable to four simple words.

"We serve rural America," Engel stated with conviction. "We do well because we do good."

That's it? That's their purpose? I thought. When Engel saw me roll my eyes, he smiled. "Let me tell you how."

"Any time you respond to a higher calling," he said, "you have an ability to produce at a much higher level. The only way to get us mere mortals to perform at a better level and act with urgency is to have a purpose and create passion around that purpose. If a business doesn't perform at a better level, they're the same as everyone else, and being the same as everyone else won't allow you to continue to have fourteen consecutive years of growth and increases in earnings. It just won't do it."

If you spend a few minutes with Engel or any other member of the CoBank team, the idea that high-speed companies with cultures of urgency and growth have a purpose to do good becomes obvious. Every employee of CoBank can convincingly explain why they work there and what their job is: to serve rural America. Ask them to expand on this purpose and each person offers up stories about funding loans so margin calls could be met, crops could be planted and cattle fed and brought to market or about how a rural telephone or water company was able to upgrade its vital services to rural businesses and communities because of a loan from CoBank. And they all know that this purpose is believed, practiced, promoted, and lived by the top brass, including Engel.

"There's no question that the leader sets the rate of the pack and is the one responsible for moving the sense of purpose of doing well by doing good throughout the company," said Engel. It's not enough to just make up a purpose that sounds good, though. "There has to be authenticity to the purpose, it has to be true, and then you have to make certain that everyone you hire understands it and buys into it." That's the real reason so many once-great organizations stumble. Their leaders get lax, hiring the wrong people and allowing circumstances to compromise their original purpose. The purpose stopped ringing true for many at Disney after 1995, at AOL after the merger with Time Warner, and even at Starbucks, which eventually led to Howard Schultz's returning to resume his role as CEO and to the subsequent greatest rising since Lazarus, which occurred because Schultz brought a purpose for doing well by doing good back into the company.

At CoBank, Engel takes pains to speak to every meeting of new associates about the thrill of serving and making rural America a better place. "I talk about purpose, why we all have jobs at CoBank, and about the higher calling we share," Engel said, "and then I tell them that if they can't wake up in the morning filled with a passion for serving rural America, which is what we do here, they shouldn't stay. I explain to them that CoBank is not a good place to come and have a job. It just isn't. It's a place to come and do something much more meaningful than a job. I also tell them that it's not for everyone." As he tells every new employee, "Life is too short to spend your time doing something you don't love. And if you don't love it, and you don't feel passionate about it, don't waste your time. But if you love serving rural America, you're in the right place."

Purpose Attracts and Ignites Everyone

Susan Vassallo, communications VP at Henry Schein, Inc., agrees with Engel on the power of purpose to attract and ignite. "It sounds corny, but I find that millennials don't want to work for just anyone," Vassallo told me. "They want to know there are good people doing good things at the company they're going to work for." Her company is another high-speed company that does well by doing good and expresses its purpose in only a few words: *advancing health care for all people.*

On the surface, Henry Schein is the world's largest distributor of health care products to dental, medical, and animal health practices. Scratch the surface and you'll find that the company, with almost $10 billion in annual revenues and more than 800,000 clients, actually provides a portfolio of solutions that allows health care providers to select the right supplies, software, equipment, pharmaceuticals, and vaccines. The company, recently named one of *Fortune*'s "most admired companies," ranks at the top in its sector, dominating with a number one rating in all nine of *Fortune*'s measured attributes: innovation, people management, use of corporate assets, social responsibility, quality of management, financial soundness, long-term investment, quality of products/services, and global competitiveness. This distinction, according to Stanley Bergman, Henry Schein's CEO and chairman, "just proves again that a company can do well by doing good. And I'm quite surprised more companies don't see the connection."

Schein initiatives like Give Kids a Smile, a partner program with the American Dental Association that's provided free dental treatment to more than 400,000 underserved children, and Prepared to Care, a fast-response program to global disasters that was first on the scene with supplies after 9/11 and Hurricane Katrina, make employees, practitioners, and manufacturers proud to be engaged in their purpose. "When I go to meetings with our people, I see they love our culture and believe in our mission, to advance health care for all people," Bergman explained. "My biggest thrill is knowing that if we can keep our culture we'll never have to worry about our financial performance."

"Health care providers all have a calling, beyond material success, to do the right thing for society," said Steve Kess, VP of global professional relations at Henry Schein. "In the past five years, we've acquired about two hundred companies globally, and when we go in, one of the ways we make it bigger and better is through our Henry Schein Cares initiatives. For example, we acquired a company in Germany, whose health care economic model is very different, more government provided. Still we found there are many niches where the need is greater than the government provides, so we empowered and facilitated programs that close those gaps. It both helps morale and helps the business grow. Doing good helps us do well."

As CoBank, Henry Schein, and hundreds of other companies of all sizes and across all industries prove, the first step to building an organization with a sense of urgency is identifying a purpose that attracts, unites, ignites, and fuels people. That purpose needs to address doing good outside the company with the inferred promise that benefits will accrue to those inside the company as well. You need to express this purpose in as few words as possible—preferably a dozen or fewer—so people can react, remember, and hopefully tell others and get them excited. If it takes more than a dozen words to explain why what you're doing is good, it will be hard for anyone inside your company, let alone outside, to remember the purpose, and you'll miss the opportunity to evoke a strong emotional connection between your company's work and doing good in the broader world. A purpose makes it clear to everyone why your company does what it does and whom and how it helps.

Feeding the Soul

In every one of my nearly one thousand keynote speeches and teaching assignments over the past dozen years, I've asked the audience a simple question: "How many of you have been on a winning team at some point in your life?"

Without exception, almost everyone raises his or her hand.

Then I walk around and ask people to share the stories of the winning teams they've been on. The head of sales for a chip manufacturer reminisces about being in a fraternity that raised $250,000 to help child burn victims. A woman who heads HR for one of the world's largest energy producers talks about her department getting together and rebuilding a home for victims of Katrina. The head of R & D for a huge social media company speaks about being on a national junior hockey team in Canada. Their eyes glisten as the memories come alive, and I probe further to prove my point. The conversations always go something like this:

"What did it feel like to be part of a winning team?"

"Terrific."

"Do you ever think about it now, all these years later?"

"Yes, all the time."

"Do you stay in touch with any of your fellow team members?"

"Yes. In fact, a few are still my best friends today."

And then the zinger: "How would you best describe that time in your life?"

"It was the best time in my life!"

Whatever their other lifetime accomplishments may have been, I'm willing to bet there is no time in their lives these people look back on more fondly than when they were united in purpose as a team, committed to doing good, to winning, and ended up doing very well.

If you're thinking, *We've already got the purpose thing wrapped up, and everyone who works for us knows what it is and buys into it*, consider the following splash of cold water.

Despite my having asked hundreds of thousands of people, "Have you ever been on a winning team?" with the exception of the companies profiled in this book, fewer than a dozen people have ever said, "Yes, I'm on one right now, here . . . *where I work.*" Clearly, the overwhelming majority of people don't find that vital sense of purpose in their work.

That's not the case at W. W. Grainger, Inc., the industrial supply company. As Jim Ryan, Grainger's CEO, proudly says, *"We help people get their job done and keep them safe. That's our purpose; it's what we do; it's why we exist."*

Ryan tells a story as an example of how this purpose plays out in the real world: "A customer walked into our Lawrence, Massachusetts, branch and needed a pair of steel-toed construction boots so he could report to work that day. We didn't have them. Our sales team leader, Rick Whitcomb, realized he wore the same size boot and said, 'Here, take mine and I'll have new ones for you tomorrow.' And when disaster strikes, acts of God or acts of man, Grainger people don't just write a check; we show up. When the planes hit on 9/11, nobody had to call. . . . Everyone just knew we'd be there and ready to serve."

Due in no small part to this shared purpose, Grainger's revenues have skyrocketed while other industrial distributors have been largely stuck in a rut. Revenues have grown at a double-digit clip and are now more than $9.4 billion annually. Under Ryan's leadership, the company's stock is up 182 percent, its market share is top in the category, and the Grainger team of 23,000 not only shows up but also sticks around, as evidenced by an average employee tenure that's twice the national average. Further, Grainger is incredibly agile and adaptable, especially when you consider it's been in the game since 1927. It's expanded product lines and regions served, now offering over a million of the essentials that keep businesses up and running safely, ten times the scope of products and expertise it had just a decade ago. Grainger is one fast company.

Every company that wants to build a quicker, more nimble organization has lots of work to do to gain this key competitive advantage. If you want to be surrounded by people who think fast and move faster, you need to provide them a good purpose so that they can become the fastest and winningest team that's ever played.

When people are invited to be part of something that they truly believe in and that has the promise of making a positive impact on people's lives, they will work doggedly, determinedly, and as fast as necessary to make things happen. As others grab hold of your purpose, they can let go of the old ways that are obstacles to new ideas. Change becomes much more manageable as people see more molehills and fewer mountain-sized obstacles in their way.

Finding Your Purpose

A sense of purpose begins with the person in charge, be it the owner, founder, CEO, or manager. Purpose might also naturally occur to a very small group of people who are about to start a venture together. Crucially, it's not something formulated by a committee and it's definitely not the result of a joined-hands kumbaya exercise conducted and voted on at an off-site retreat. If your business requires a committee to answer the question "Why do we *really* do what we do and what's the *good* we're trying to accomplish," you've missed the point. Finding your purpose occurs when your head and heart meet.

"It begins as a lump in the throat," said Robert Frost, "a sense of wrong, a homesickness, a lovesickness." Frost was talking about his purpose as one of the world's greatest poets, but his words perfectly mirror what I've heard from purpose-driven executives.

For Stan Bergman, Henry Schein's CEO, purpose came from growing up in South Africa during apartheid. "My parents made sure I knew what was going on, as the government was quite good at insulating white people from the reality of their policies," he said about identifying his sense of right and wrong. "I got to see the evil of apartheid right in front of me and compare it to the good I saw my father, a doctor, do to help others. Thankfully for me, what you see at home is what drives you. So when I came to the U.S. and was introduced to Henry Schein, I saw what the former owners were doing to make a difference in the world. They were all extremely generous and involved in many causes. The company led the effort to help change generic-drug laws, making lifesaving drugs available for more people, among many other noble efforts. That connected with me. All of us at Henry Schein feel the sense of wrong and are alert to the injustices of our society, and fixing those injustices became our common purpose, along with a commitment to our customers, suppliers, and investors and to growth."

Mike McCallister, chairman and former CEO of health insurance giant Humana, shares this view of purpose. "You might think that what we have here is a health insurance company, but it really isn't," he said. "It's a front for what we're really trying to do, which is *completely change and reinvent the world of health care.*"

McCallister saw something wrong with how people interacted with and benefited from health care, so he put all his heart into fixing it. With this strong sense of purpose, McCallister was able in a very short time to take Humana, a troubled company whose value had slipped to $700 million following a disastrous merger, and grow it to a market capitalization of almost $13 billion, expanding the workforce from 14,000 regional employees to 45,000 employees providing insurance services in all fifty states.

Ron Sargent, the highly successful CEO of Staples, shares this understanding of purpose as a higher good. When he told me about what purpose meant to him and to the 74,000 Staples employees, Sargent became misty-eyed. Staples' purpose, which it refers to as its soul, is "joining diversity, the environment, our community and ethics."

That might sound surprising to those who believe that Staples' purpose is to sell office supplies, but it's true.

"Think about how important a job is to somebody in my hometown of Covington, Kentucky, and then consider that we've created 74,000 of them," Sargent points out. "My coworkers tell me all the time, 'My Staples stock options bought me a home' or 'My

Staples stock put my kids through college' or 'I'm going to retire because of the great life I've had at Staples.'"

"Those are the things that bring tears to your eyes," Sargent said. "When I was a kid, I never dreamed about growing up and selling office supplies; selling office supplies is boring. But when you think about what you're allowed to create as a result of that, the people, the jobs, and the good that comes from running a big business and doing real well, it's more than humbling."

Likewise, Fred Eppinger, president and CEO of Hanover Insurance, has succeeded by leading with a purpose. Eppinger took charge of his hometown company after it had been critically wounded by former leadership, severely downgraded by the industry rating organizations, and blasted by critics who questioned whether the company could survive. Hanover Insurance had shrunk in ten of the previous eleven years, dabbled in businesses it had no expertise in, and devolved into a bureaucracy. To make matters worse, Eppinger learned he had a looming $2 billion liability on his hands (due to misguided annuity sales promoted by his predecessor) that was a ticking time bomb.

Bad as those things were, each was a business problem he'd seen and fixed before as a consultant and leading troubleshooter for McKinsey & Company. Eppinger was well prepared to tackle the problems head on. But within a month of taking over at Hanover, he learned what was really wrong.

"One of the associates was at a Christmas party for her husband's company and someone asked where she worked," Eppinger said. "She wouldn't say Hanover Insurance because it was so embarrassing." Eppinger interviewed other employees about how they felt about Hanover. That same word—"embarrassed"—came up a lot.

That's when Eppinger figured out what was truly wrong: a lack of purpose that could hold the company together. "You can't get the best out of people who are embarrassed to be with you," he said. So Eppinger boldly promised everyone that they'd "never, never, never be embarrassed again! I talked to them about our purpose of *being here to take care of people when something horrible happens,* talked about our journey and announced we were doubling our donations to the community and showed them how we were going to make a difference. Making everyone proud became a huge part of our purpose."

Eppinger got rid of the leaders who didn't buy into the purpose and quickly assembled a team of people who believed the same thing he did. Together they quickly got the company back on its feet by uniting the workforce through purpose: ridding themselves of that $2 billion liability, tripling revenues, and quadrupling the company's share price.

Purpose Fuels Urgency

A strong purpose isn't just about making a point of doing good. It also fuels urgency. A group of people who share a purpose of doing something good can't wait to make it happen, to get it to their prospective customers, to make an impact, to make something better and in the process make the world a slightly better place. There's no need to urge associates to *hurry up.* Speed occurs naturally when a group of people share a strong sense of purpose about doing something good.

Almost every company in existence was born out of someone's having a purpose wrapped around doing something good. The problem is that, as time goes on, most people start taking the continuation of the business for granted and inevitably the day-to-day routine, posturing, and politics begin taking precedence and either the purpose is forgotten or the bureaucrats cut the guts out of it and replace it with wordy vision and mission statements. When that happens, the passion, the real reason for speed, disappears.

CREATING AND CASCADING PURPOSE

As the leader of a large company, a small business, an entrepreneurial start-up, or a division within a company, you can find your purpose by reflecting on why the company was founded or on a moment when the company did something good or touched a customer in a profound way. Was it something a customer said? Are you remembering a time you swooped in and made a bad situation better? Did you help someone and change their life? Was it an accomplishment the cynics said was impossible? Or was it just reflecting on how you took your people somewhere they really wanted to go? The leader holds the establishment and protection of purpose in his hand, though the team has to support and execute.

Keep It Brief

Once you have thought about the purpose that unites your company and marks why you do what you do, you have to come up with a way to articulate and share it with others. You must be able to state your purpose clearly to another person and evoke a strong emotional reaction in only a few words. Unless you can make someone's eyes light up and get to him or her to say, "Aha, I get what you're talking about," and elect to follow you or not, either you're using too many words or your heart was absent when you formulated your purpose.

Don't make the mistake of thinking the vision or mission statement your company already has is sufficient. People don't remember, take ownership of, or act in the interests of traditional vision and mission statements as we've come to know them. I know that firsthand.

Several years ago, while serving on the board of directors of a large charitable organization, I took part in a multiday board retreat. During the day, we conducted our business in a large conference room. Hanging in front of the room were two large banners, each with a few paragraphs of type on them, one titled "Our Vision" and the other, "Our Mission." All week those banners were up there for us to look at and absorb.

During the final day's lunch break, I sneaked into the room and removed the banners. When everyone returned after the break, I stood up and told the group of fifteen board members that I'd donate $1,000 to the charity for each person who could correctly write the organization's vision and mission statements on a piece of paper. Not a single person, including board members who had served the organization for years and even the organization's CEO, was able to even come close to remembering the long, generic babble—even though they were the very ones who had written it!

Make It Memorable

Colleen Cervantes is the president of Chevron Lubricants, a large operating division within the $220 billion energy giant. The first time we spoke, I began by asking her to tell me about the division she leads. (I didn't want to signal that I knew nothing about her field!)

Luckily Cervantes is, by nature, an enthusiast—and she knows her company's purpose well enough that she was able to get an "aha" out of me within moments. All she had to say was "We make the stuff that makes the whole world run," adding, "Without lubricants, every piece of equipment in the world would eventually stop."

Clearly, Cervantes understands the vital need to unite diverse groups of people all around the world with a strong sense of purpose. By the time we'd completed our conversation, I wanted to go back to school, get a degree in engineering, and join her team. While I can't necessarily imagine a life's work spent in lubricants, I can easily imagine being proud of a life spent making the stuff that makes the whole world run. That's an organization and a leader who know how to articulate their purpose.

Way back in 1930, Mike Cullen, an employee of Kroger Foods, wrote a letter to the company's president, Bernard Kroger, proposing a new type of store called a supermarket that would offer low prices on consumables but wouldn't offer delivery or allow customers to charge their groceries to store accounts. With these changes, Cullen believed that a supermarket could do ten times the sales and profits of the typical small Kroger or A&P store. He never received an acknowledgment or answer from Kroger, so he took his life savings and moved his family to Long Island, where he opened America's first supermarket (according to the Smithsonian Institution). Almost ninety years later, the family still owns thirty-nine King Kullen stores in Queens, New York, doing $1 billion in annual revenues.

What gave Cullen, his family, and his employees the grit they needed to revolutionize the grocery industry? A clear purpose: "to become the world's greatest price wrecker." Pretty memorable stuff, right?

SHOW DEEP CONVICTION

Five Catholic nuns, known as the Sisters of St. Mary's, traveled from Germany to St. Louis in 1872 to be of service to sick people in need. When people couldn't afford to pay for the health care they received, the nuns simply recorded them in journals as "Our

Dear Lord's" and never asked for payment. The charity of those sisters inspired powerful words that are in the hearts and on the lips of all thirty thousand medical professionals at what is now known as SSM Health Care: "Through exceptional health care services we reveal the healing presence of God."

SSM Health Care is a remarkable group of 20 acute-care hospitals and 150 outpatient sites in America's Midwest. It was the first U.S. health care organization to receive the Malcolm Baldrige National Quality Award, the only formal recognition of performance excellence of both public and private U.S. organizations given by the president of the United States. I've heard a few giggles and seen some eyes roll when I've told audiences about this extraordinary company and repeated its purpose, but that doesn't concern me—nor does it concern the leaders at SSM.

A purpose is not supposed to appeal to 100 percent of all people. If you have the right one, in fact, it's the best screening device for finding the right workforce and the right customers. If they giggle, they're a bad bet. But if they understand your focused purpose, they're probably the right people to work with you or for you to work for.

It's Great to Be Foolish

Whenever I need to quickly check that a purpose is big and bold enough to attract, unite, ignite, and maintain the momentum of an organization, I remember the words of wisdom shared in Tim Burton's movie *Big Fish*. Albert Finney, as Edward Bloom Senior, says something that rings true about purpose: "There's a time when a man needs to fight and a time when he needs to accept that his destiny is lost, the ship has sailed, and that only a *fool* would continue. Truth is," he tells his son, "I've always been a fool."

Charlie Chaplin was a fool for his art; nothing could deter him. Henry Ford's investors called him a fool for believing that every family would own a car. The board fired Steve Jobs for wanting to change the way the world computed, enjoyed music, and communicated. Jonas Salk was a fool for a vaccine and Lady Gaga for her music.

What's big enough and important enough to you that you're willing to look (or feel) foolish for persisting and persevering?

Childhood buddies Bill Gates and Paul Allen founded Microsoft when they created the first programming language for the Altair 8800 computer and ignited the microcomputing revolution. Their purpose with Microsoft was simple; they were determined to *put a computer with Microsoft software on every desk in the world.* They imagined a world that would be a better place when everyone had access to data, and they used their purpose to get others to join them. That certainly sounded foolishly big at the time!

Microsoft's growing workforce, passionate about the dream of making the world a better place, worked night and day to chase their purpose, occasionally catching a few hours of sleep in their cubicles and then starting all over again. Within only a few years, their speed resulted in the company's going public, in the process creating three billionaires and more than twelve thousand employee millionaires.

For years Microsoft was the most innovative high-tech company on the planet and then, as soon as it started taking its success and predictable cash flow for granted, it lost the plot. This happens frequently when companies lose sight of doing well by doing good. After only a few months on the job, in July 2014, new Microsoft CEO, Satya Nadella, wrote a three-thousand-word e-mail to all of the company's employees in which he identified the source of this discontent. "We need to rediscover our soul," he wrote, making it clear that the company's future existed in doing well by doing good. "Our mission is not to deliver software products but *to develop technology to help people live better lives.*"

Remember, It's a Journey

All Ingvar Kamprad had when he started IKEA in 1943 were two empty hands and a purpose: "To create a better everyday life for the many." Amazingly, almost seventy years later, when I interview scores of executives and designers to learn about the magic that has made IKEA the world's only global furniture brand and Kamprad one of the ten wealthiest people in the world, everyone I speak to tells me how they made Kamprad's purpose their own.

One common element of all good purposes is that they are a lasting inspiration, able to guide strategy and suggest hundreds of thousands of goals. But no purpose is ever finished; there's always a need for the next step and the next brilliant innovation. A purpose should be big enough to fill a lifetime of work, offer something to strive for each day, and never quite be fully attained because there's always more to do, while still providing fulfillment and satisfaction every day.

Get Your Senior Team On Board

There's an old African proverb that says, "If you want to go fast, go alone, but if you want to go far, go together." In order to be urgent and maintain velocity, everyone in the organization must be joined as one in pursuit of the good the organization is trying to achieve.

Google's founders, Larry Page and Sergey Brin, started their company with the purpose of *organizing all the information in the* *world and never doing evil.* Google wouldn't have gotten off the ground and become one of the world's most successful companies if one cofounder had said of the other, "Well, he's got this idea about organizing all the information in the world and never doing evil, but frankly, I think that's b*&@%^t and to me it's just about the money." Unless all the senior leaders believe and are seen as believing in the same thing, the company will eventually become filled with discord and subversion and eventually go off the rails or implode.

Hire Only Those Who Believe in the Good You're Trying to Do

James Archer borrowed $50,000 to found Multi-Chem, an incredibly lucrative oil services company that he sold in 2013 for $650 million. Archer credits the company's workforce for its success, and he's not wrong. But when you dig a little deeper, you learn that the organization was as successful as it was because of its extraordinary, dedicated hiring practices. Everyone who joined the company did so after being interviewed five times, to make certain he or she fervently believed in Archer's purpose for the company: to provide unparalleled local customer service.

Archer's commandment was "hire hard and manage easy." "When you hire people of integrity," he says, "who are capable of doing the job, want to be part of what you're trying to do, and share your purpose, you don't need a lot of rules. Rules are for the 2 percent of people who need them. We'd just rather weed those people out before hiring them."

Amazon, whose purpose about doing well by doing good is to be *the earth's most customer-centric company,* screens recruits through several hundred "bar raisers" who work for the company. These people have full-time jobs but volunteer (for no extra compensation) to interview as many as ten potential employees weekly in interviews lasting two to three hours apiece. Anyone being considered for a leadership position in the company will be interviewed by several bar raisers; any one of them can veto a hiring, even if their own expertise has nothing to do with the skill sets being sought. The program's objective is to make certain that people being hired are not only qualified but also fast thinkers, adaptable, and committed to the culture and purpose of the company. Think about that: cultural screening by the culture itself.

Shine a Light on the Good You're Doing

Various studies estimate that between tweets, e-mails, texts, mass media commercials, Web, print, and outdoor ads, people are subjected to between three hundred and two thousand impressions daily battling for their attention. Companies with a purpose built around doing something good are always searching for stories and examples of how they're living the purpose and then sharing those stories with others.

When Charles Schwab was in the processing of quickly growing his company into the largest personal financial services/brokerage company in the world, he went on a hiring binge. His organization's big challenge was getting new recruits up to speed on and enrolling them as believers in the culture. At every off-site company meeting, the manager would place a rocking chair on the stage and spend an hour having people sit in the chair and tell their favorite stories of how Schwab had helped people realize their financial dreams.

Great CEOs, owners, managers, and executives constantly remind people about the good the company does.

Celebrate Your Purpose

You've probably heard this expression before: "Heroes aren't braver, they're just brave longer." Most of us easily get derailed long before we face any life-threatening dangers. How can some people muster such grit and maintain their urgency and commitment? It's as simple as being recognized and applauded.

Research conducted by Matthew Lieberman and Liz Castle in the United States and Keise Izuma in Japan confirms that our brains crave positive feedback. Being thanked or praised, it turns out, is as much of a physical reward as a scoop of our favorite dessert. Adam Grant, professor at Wharton and author of *Give and Take,* and David Rock of the NeuroLeadership Institute have also conducted research that looks at how appreciation affects people. They found that many people will actually trade money for hearing they are appreciated.

Parties and celebrations are an incredible tactic, one that most leaders fail to make a priority. It's not only a motivator; it's also a teacher. When you hear of others' great accomplishments, you see yourself doing the same things to get that rush from recognition.

Give People the Why and They'll Give You the How

The purpose of a business, we were taught, was to make money and grind out a profit because profit is how you give a fair return to investors and because you need profit to grow. Unless you make that profit, your business will cease to exist.

It made sense but it seemed so hollow.

Harvard professor Theodore Levitt wrote a revolutionary takedown of those who teach profit as the ultimate "purpose" of a business. In his book *The Marketing Imagination,* Levitt explained that profit is to a company as breakfast, lunch, and dinner are to a man or woman. Levitt concluded, while everyone must eat to live, if you *live to eat*, you'll end up living a life that is empty and unhappy.

Purpose is something bigger and better, and in a high-speed company it becomes a uniting, motivating, soul-satisfying reason for all our hard work and the inspiration to overcome obstacles. As Gandhi said, having a mighty purpose and changing the world are connected: "Our thoughts become our words, our words become our actions, our actions become our character, and our character becomes our destiny."

If you want to build and lead an enterprise with a culture of urgency and growth, the only proper and logical starting point is to begin by making certain that everyone knows and believes the company's purpose, the *why*. It will change your destiny. Bob Engel, CoBank's CEO, said it best in sharing his insightful observations on purpose: "When people know and buy into the *why*, they'll figure out the *how*." Let's make this our mantra as we learn how to set up a purpose-driven, fast-moving organization.

FAST TASKS

- Take a walk through your company and ask twelve people—preferably people you don't know or work directly with—to recite, without prompting, the company's vision and mission statements. You'll be surprised and humbled.
- Use the guidelines presented in this chapter to compose the twelve words (or fewer) that describe the real purpose of your business, one that allows the enterprise to do well by doing good.

- Once you begin living the purpose in everything you do and every decision you make, it's time to get people on board—one person at a time, top to bottom. By the time the top levels of the company are seen as being on board with a purpose of doing good, others will start getting on board . . . or leave, which is exactly what you want to happen. A good purpose is contagious.

CHAPTER TWO
Principles and Values

THE "SHALLS" AND "SHALL NOTS" OF SPEED

I was in the United lounge in Denver, waiting for my delayed flight home and speaking with the CEO of a Silicon Valley manufacturer. It was one of those maddening rolling delays where the departure time just keeps getting pushed back and the airline tells you less and less. Over a few beers, our conversation covered a lot of ground and then took a surprising turn.

"You're the guy that writes books on strategy," he said, with a slight edge to his voice. "So answer one question for me: How do companies stay strategic?"

"What do you mean *stay* strategic?" I asked.

"We start every year with a well-thought-out strategy in place," he said. "But as soon as crap starts happening or we're having a bad month, we start doing whatever we have to do to slam stuff out the door, the plan goes out the window, and we're right back where we started and grab at whatever we need to do in order to hit our numbers. We lose the plot!"

Then he said something he'd have never confessed to the financial analysts who followed his company. "Our inability to stay focused on our long-term strategy and the fact that we do stupid things to try and hit our numbers always come back and bite us in the ass. It drives me nuts, puts us at risk, and ends up slowing everything down."

"If you're willing to play along with me," I said, "you'll have the answer you're seeking."

"We're not going anywhere soon," he replied, "so play away."

"Imagine you're a military leader commanding a coalition at war. After many tough battles, victory is in sight, and the only thing your forces need to do to win is take control of the opponent's last stronghold. What would your big objective be?" I asked.

"That's a no-brainer," he said. "You'd want to win the war as fast as possible."

"Before deciding how you're going to take out the enemy's last stronghold," I continued, "here's some information for you. The city occupied by the enemy clings to the side of a high mountain and is inaccessible by tanks or armored troop carriers. Vast resources have been expended to get your forces to the brink of victory, your troops are exhausted, and you want to end the war quickly and go home victorious. Here's the big question: What would you do to defeat the enemy and claim victory?"

"There are lots of things you could do," he said. "You could bomb the village and end things quickly or you could wait them out. You could negotiate surrender, poison their water, launch an all-out airborne assault, or infiltrate the village with your forces."

"That's true," I said. "But what if I told you that the enemy is holding two hundred young children hostage? Now which options would you choose?"

He thought for a minute, hemmed and hawed, then replied. "That changes things. I guess you'd take bombing, poisoning, and the assault off the table."

"Why would you take those options off the table?"

"Well, unless you're some kind of Dr. Strangelove," he said, "your principles, or I guess what you'd call your values, wouldn't allow the harming of hundreds of young children, so you'd probably opt to wait them out, negotiate, or infiltrate the village."

I explained that in the story I'd just told him there were three key elements that every organization needs: a big strategic objective, a list of possible tactics to achieve it, and a set of guiding principles (guiding values) by which to select the right tactics. Based on what he'd told me, his company was missing the most important one of the three. I promised that if he scratched his head and thought hard about the story, he would figure out what was missing and, in doing so, could come up with a way to stop being tactical and be strategically fast.

I excused myself for a moment to check on the flight, saw that it would finally be boarding in a few minutes, and went back to say good-bye. We exchanged business cards, shook hands, and promised to stay in touch, though we never did. I've wondered if he figured out what was missing at his company. Seeing the bad financial news and press in the year that followed, and the eventual announcement that he was leaving to "pursue other interests and move back to Colorado," I'm concluding he never did.

What was missing in my airport acquaintance's company was a clear set of guiding principles by which the *right* decisions could be made quickly and naturally. Without guiding principles, companies end up clutching any available tactic in order to try to hit their numbers. Just as you would never build a house without a foundation because it would topple, trying to have a culture of urgency without a set of guiding values will ensure only that the company is in constant turmoil and eventually will careen out of control.

Faster, Smarter Decisions

As Moses delivered Christianity and Judaism a list of "thou shalls" and "thou shall nots," Buddha provided Buddhists an eightfold path, Muhammad gave Islam the five pillars, and Patañjali gave the Hindus their five principles and ten disciplines, it's the responsibility of the leader in any culture to provide his or her organization with a set of guiding values. Only through these values can the *right* day-to-day decisions be made and acted upon quickly by associates at every level, especially on the front lines.

High-speed companies don't need to waste time in long, drawn-out meetings where everyone shares their carefully rehearsed and self-important points of view in order to make a decision. Their employees can meet standing in the hallway for a few minutes, make a quick decision, and get on with it. Leaders in these companies don't wring their hands and study things to death; it can be a quick yes or no. Companies that think and move urgently don't lose time sending things out to committees for evaluation. They're too busy with the important work—growth—of the company.

Decisions are made more quickly in fast companies because their people begin with a purpose that serves as their big strategic objective. They also have a set of guiding principles by which they can rapidly select the tactics they're going to use to accomplish their big strategic objective. Those three key elements break down like this:

- The strategic objective is the big thing the business is trying to achieve that explains where it's headed and what it's trying to be. It might be to be "the best Italian restaurant in Kansas," "the most respected financial services firm in the nation," or "the number one self-help medical app in the world." You need only one big strategic objective.

- Tactics are the actions that will be used by a company to achieve the big strategic objective. Tactics should never be confused with strategy. Companies can have hundreds of tactics to choose from, depending on circumstances. Most companies also waste precious time and resources discussing, studying, developing, selecting, and reinventing tactical responses to the same old challenges. Unless you have a set of guiding principles, every decision must be made, agonizingly, from scratch.

- Guiding principles are rules that leaders use to select the tactics they're going to use. Think of them as the "shalls" and "shall nots" of the company culture that keep everyone true to their stated purpose.

If you're breathing a sigh of relief because your company already has the "guiding principles" element taken care of, don't fool yourself. There's a 99.999 percent chance your company doesn't actually have a good or firm understanding of this.

Of the 220,000 companies we've screened and studied over the years, we identified fewer than *two dozen* where everyone knew the company's guiding principles and used them when making tactical decisions. It's not enough that your company sent out the values memo and posted the values on a Web site. Until everyone truly knows the guiding principles or values, believes and understands them, is empowered to act in accordance with them, and works in a transparent system that ensures those principles are used at every level religiously, all you have is a collection of pretty, politically correct words that won't make your company faster. Only when *everyone* in your organization understands and buys into the big strategic objective and knows and makes *all decisions* in accordance with the guiding principles can your company naturally be more nimble in executing the tactics you select.

One great example of a company where everyone knows the guiding principles is CoBank (whose purpose we explored in chapter 1). As Engel explains it, "I tell our people repeatedly to measure decisions against one guiding value: Does the decision you're making and the direction you're taking feel like *I know more and care more about the customer than any other financial institution?* If it feels that way, then you're making a good choice. If it doesn't, think about doing something different."

Nucor Steel builds from its guiding principles as well and lets those values steer its tactical and strategic behavior. The North Carolina–based company is the nation's largest steelmaker thanks to its breakthroughs in making error-free, injury-free steel in mere minutes. It has also increased the quarterly dividend it has paid its shareholders for 160 consecutive quarters, a feat achieved by only fourteen other companies in the world. And it's never had a layoff.

Nucor is able to think and act quickly because it has strong guiding principles. Everyone in the company, from CEO John Ferriola on down, knows these rules and lives by them, setting their strategic objectives and making their tactical decisions against the following values. Imagine how much easier and faster decision making is when you have a set of rules like these:

NUCOR STEEL'S GUIDING PRINCIPLES

- We'll produce steel in a constantly more efficient and environmentally friendly way.
- Our employees are our only asset.
- Employees, neighbors, and shareholders will always be treated fairly.
- Decisions will all be made on long-term survival, not short-term gains.
- Management will always be accessible and accountable.
- Everyone will conduct themselves according to the highest ethical standards.
- We won't have layoffs and we'll keep the right people on the team even in tough economies.
- The best idea wins.

The Value of Guiding Principles

Companies with sets of guiding principles and values that are known and practiced by everyone in the organization are significantly faster at decision making. This helps foster a sense of speed and getting things done quickly within the entire company. Here's why:

Provides Predictability

Uncertainty is greater than ever; it's true across every industry and not likely to change. No one knows what markets or the economy will look like a few months or a year out, there's no lifetime guarantee of a job, and a month from now you might be working for a new owner. Most people are rightfully insecure about their future prospects. But a set of shared guiding values provides all people within your company one thing they can count on: Everyone from top to bottom is playing by the same set of rules.

When companies dart feverishly from tactic to tactic, the uncertainty that results causes people to instinctively slow down and become guarded. Instead of working on the strategic objective, they start looking out for themselves. Guiding principles remind people that there is safety and strength in unity. As Benjamin Franklin said at the signing of the Declaration of Independence—in advice equally suited to leaders and managers—"We must all hang together, or assuredly we shall all hang separately." The *right* set of guiding principles assures people that their value will be recognized, that their sacrifice will lead to reward, and that the company can be trusted to do the right thing. Guiding principles tell everyone that "we'll hang together and play by the same rules despite uncertainty." A few stakes in the ground provide a sense of assurance and predictability, allowing everyone to focus on the important work at hand.

Eliminates Bureaucracy and Micromanagement

Seven out of ten employees say the most stressful part of their job is dealing with their boss. The reason for this tension, research shows, is "unnecessary leadership" or what most of us call bureaucracy and micromanaging.

You can't actually do everyone's thinking for them. You're not that smart, and if you happen to be that smart, your people will resent your micromanagement so much that they'll move heaven and earth to prove you wrong. Leadership is the art of improving everyone's execution without undue supervising, surveillance, or pestering.

Guiding values create your specific boundaries. When the senior leadership and management team know that all decisions will be made by everyone in accordance with the set of shalls and shall nots they created, they'll naturally become more comfortable with decisions being made by people beneath them in the organizational structure. A set of guiding principles reduces the number of excuses for unproductive micromanagement, lets people focus on doing their part, and moves decision making down to the lowest levels.

Ends Paralysis by Analysis

The age of big data, of having all the facts and figures we could possibly want at our fingertips, promises more security than it can deliver. It lulls us into the false belief that getting more information means no chance of making any missteps.

Big companies invest 200,000 employee hours per billion dollars in revenue generating yearly forecasts and budgets. That means companies like Blockbuster, Borders, Circuit City, Sears, HP, and Sprint spent millions of hours analyzing and planning. Did all that data make them successful? Of course not. Blockbuster, Borders, and Circuit City went bankrupt or disappeared while Sears, HP, RadioShack, and Sprint currently do little more than limp along. They used that data the same way a drunk uses a lamppost: as something to hold on to for support instead of illumination.

Running a business is a lot like crossing white water by jumping from rock to rock. Experimentation, making a lot of small bets, and learning in quick action loops while focused on the big objective will lead to better outcomes than time spent generating extravagant plans. Guiding principles encourage that engagement and action.

Increases Cooperation and Coordination

Over the last decade, over eleven thousand executives have shared their concerns and frustrations with me and my research team. One common frustration we hear across industries is the challenge of aligning agendas and keeping everyone on the same page. "Our bonuses and incentive plans aren't enough," we're told. "We need something more than bonus plans to keep everyone communicating, coordinating, and cooperating."

Having a shared purpose and a shared set of guiding values turns workforces into communities of people who have chosen to be part of a culture, speak a common language, and are trying to accomplish the same things. When I visited a Nucor Steel plant in Utah, I was shocked to see workers whose shifts wouldn't begin for another hour gathered in small groups around their cars with members of their team, sharing coffee, sandwiches, and conversation. When I asked the plant manager why they'd shown up an hour before they'd go on the clock, he smiled and said, "That happens before every shift. But they don't show up early to BS. They're figuring out how to increase their paychecks by making more error-free steel today than they did yesterday." Everyone showing up an hour early to coordinate and align their agendas is the kind of cooperation most owners and managers can only dream about.

Increases Transparency

The act of publishing principles sets up accountability and transparency. It gives all your people a yardstick. When management (from headquarters or down the chain of command) falls short, they see it and can tell you about it. It takes courage to publish such a list, but also it makes a lot of sense. When would you prefer to learn your leadership is falling short: before or after your best customers and best employees are thoroughly disappointed in you?

Under the leadership of CEO Jack Welch, GE had five guiding principles: "Be number one or number two or be sold off," "Live quality," "Live speed," "Constantly focus on innovation," and "Behave like a small company."

One of Welch's great growth accomplishments came when some midlevel managers brazenly told top executives that one of Welch's cherished principles had been taken to "nonsensical levels." In 1995 Welch heard that managers were taking the principle of "be number one or number two or be sold off" to extremes by redefining and narrowing the industry they were in, in order to ensure that they were ranked number one or two. In order to be number one or two in a narrowly defined industry group and save their departments from cuts, managers were passing up growth opportunities that would expand the definition of their industry. Welch called the criticism from these midlevel managers "a punch in the nose" that caused him to reconsider this principle. Because of the managers' critique, Welch relaxed his rule, and the new broader definition of the principle became what Welch later called a major factor in GE's acceleration to double-digit growth.

Gives Everyone a Moral Compass

Back in 2002, Bristol-Myers Squibb Company was accused of boosting business through questionable tactics, including channel stuffing (jamming additional products into distributors' hands to artificially pump up sales), restructuring reserves and making repeated asset sales to bolster operating profits, and taking excessive write-offs. I don't share this with you to denigrate the company; I know it denied the accusations and paid some huge fines. I share this story with you because these kinds of things can happen and have happened in other companies because senior employees were not provided a clear moral compass.

The best defense against unethical tactics starts with a well-defined and transparent set of guiding values. Your people need to be told there are lines you shall not cross, there is behavior that is not acceptable, and no matter how dire the financial situation, there are certain tactics you shall not employ.

A written set of guiding principles that set the boundaries and transparency are your early-warning system for transgressions. Make your principles the one subject that is not part of any chain-of-command protocols. Encourage everyone to check your moral compass and report anyone who veers off course to your office if necessary. Remember, if you don't say something is forbidden, you've really said *anything goes*.

Enables Faster Adaptation

The greatest threat to your growth doesn't come from competitors, a bad economy, or random acts of God. The greatest threat comes from inside your company.

Hanging on to old thinking, allowing turf wars to fester, or investing precious resources on yesterday's breadwinners has damaged or killed far more companies than the last eight recessions. There is perhaps no better example of a company falling prey to this mentality than Blockbuster.

When Netflix started sending customers videos through the mail and cable and phone companies started streaming films, Blockbuster couldn't figure out how to respond. If one of its guiding principles had addressed offering exceptional customer satisfaction, it would have been ahead of Netflix and the phone and cable companies. Instead, its only apparent principle was to screw their customers and earn greater profits by way of late fees and add on selling of candy or salty snacks. Until the bitter end Blockbuster thought its competitors were other video-rental chains. Meanwhile, Netflix swooped in and destroyed its business before Blockbuster knew what hit it.

Bad generals always fight the last war. The same is true of managers who do the same thing expecting different results. It's called methodism, the unthinking application of the same routine(s) to every situation, and it is a crippling flaw among decision makers. Guiding principles encourage everyone to "adapt, improvise, and overcome" with the speed and precision of the best warriors.

Never Get in a Jam with Guiding Principles

When I was researching my book *Hit the Ground Running: A Manual for New Leaders,* I set out to learn how some new leaders are able to figure out what's wrong with their company, find the right people, plan the right moves, and inspire thousands to put their hearts into getting everything done quickly while most new leaders get stuck at square one or two.

My research team and I analyzed 370 new CEOs who headed *Fortune* 1000 companies during a specific time frame and identified those whose performances were at the very top of the heap. We found twelve leaders, including Jeff Lorberbaum of Mohawk Industries, Marshall Larsen of Goodrich, and Howard Lance of Harris Corporation, who pulled off the most impressive transformations faster and better than all the other new CEOs, and we asked them how they did it.

Looking back, I realize that they showed us far more than the strategies that had allowed them to successfully double revenues, triple earnings, and take net profit margins to new heights in record time. These leaders actually shared their simple guiding principles for creating a culture of urgency and growth. Each principle was easy to understand, incredibly wise, and thoroughly battle tested.

One of the companies we identified and studied is the best example you'll find of an enterprise that has achieved and maintained lightning-fast velocity. You'd never guess that a company that's been around for more than a hundred years and is best known for jams and jellies would offer a truly incredible example of urgency and thinking and moving fast.

Under the leadership of Tim and Richard Smucker, J.M. Smucker has not only enjoyed significant organic growth but also quickly gobbled up and grown such iconic brands as Folgers, Dunkin' Donuts coffee products, Pillsbury, Hungry Jack, Carnation, Knott's, and Jif. These folks, headquartered in tiny Orrville, Ohio, are fast. Between 2004 and 2014, they grew revenues ten times, from $600 million to $6 billion, and introduced an average of fifty new products a year, growing profits by almost 800 percent.

The Smuckers instinctively knew that a culture of urgency and growth needs leaders who are never seen as unappreciative, distracted, discouraging, or depressing. They followed their father's deceptively simple recipe to supervise positively: "Say thank you for a job well done, listen with your full attention, look for the good in others, and have a sense of humor." As counterintuitive as it might seem to cynics, the Smuckers have proved that when you truly appreciate and thank people, actually listen to them, have a sense of humor, and provide them with a set of guiding principles, they'll bend over backward to help you be faster. As one of the supervisors told me as I was touring the company's Orrville plant, "I've been thanked more in the one year I've worked here than in the nine years I spent in my last job. I'd do anything for these people."

This spirit of appreciation and these incredible results are clearly traceable to the company's well-defined guiding principles. Everyone who works for J.M. Smucker can recite the company's five basic beliefs. Imagine the power of having everyone who works with and for you being able to do the same.

THE J.M. SMUCKER COMPANY'S BASIC BELIEFS

Quality

Quality applies to our products, manufacturing methods, marketing efforts, people, and our relationships with each other.

The Smucker family of brands will continue to be known as the highest quality products offered. We only produce and sell products that enhance the quality of life and well-being. We continuously look for daily improvements that will, over time, result in consistently superior products and performance. Our growth and business success have been built on a foundation of quality, earning the trust of our constituents in our products and our people. At Smucker, quality will continue to come first.

Ethics

The same strong ethical values on which our company was founded provide the standards by which we conduct our business, as well as ourselves.

These values include honesty, respect, trust, responsibility, and fairness. We accept nothing less, regardless of the circumstances. Therefore, we maintain the highest standard of ethics with our consumers, customers, employees, suppliers, communities, and shareholders.

People

We seek employees with integrity who are committed to preserving and enhancing the values and principles inherent in our *Basic Beliefs* through their own actions.

We are fair with our employees and maintain an environment that encourages personal responsibility within the company and the community. In return, we expect our employees to be responsible for not only their individual jobs but for the company as a whole.

Growth

Along with day-to-day operations, we continuously look forward and focus on the potential of our company. Growing is reaching for that potential, whether through the acquisition of new brands, development of new products and new markets, the discovery of new management or manufacturing capabilities, or the personal growth and development of our people and their ideas.

Growth also requires that we maintain a global perspective of the world in which we conduct business and a responsibility for our impact on the cultural, economic, environmental, and social fabric of our global community. We are committed to strong, balanced growth within prudent financial parameters. This balanced growth will enable us to both provide a fair return to our shareholders and enhance our consumer franchise. We remain independent from short-term, external influences because we believe that when we make decisions with a long-term perspective, growth will naturally follow.

Independence

We have a strong commitment to the stewardship of the company. We strive to be an example of a company that can achieve success while conducting business in accordance with our *Basic Beliefs*. We believe that the interests of all of our constituents—consumers, customers, employees, suppliers, communities, and shareholders—are best served by preserving the unique Smucker culture and maintaining our independence.

We strongly believe that our proven track record of creating long-term value has been built on the foundation of our culture and independence. To us, value means bringing families together, building brands that are among the most trusted with consumers and customers, investing in our communities, developing our people, and, ultimately, delivering long-term returns to our shareholders.

Guiding principles are stakes in the ground that create boundaries that keep organizations strategic rather than tactical. Facing tough competition, potential disasters, business units needing a complete makeover, and all the uncertainty that keeps every manager tossing and turning at night, companies that think fast and move faster are able to do what's best for the short term and the long run.

CREATING AND CASCADING YOUR GUIDING PRINCIPLES

J.M Smucker's guiding principles are a good example of what your organization's guiding principles should look like. They should be simply stated and easy for everyone to understand but based on tremendous underlying wisdom. Each should be broad enough to guide actions at every level from the shop floor to the C suite yet specific enough that people can see where they are accountable. They should be inspirational and memorable enough to make your people proud of this call to action.

Make a Short List

You don't need more than five or six guiding principles. People won't remember more than that—and there probably aren't more than five or six things worthy of inclusion. State each guiding principle in as few words as possible and then hang some flesh on the bones with a brief explanation that provides context.

Buy-in at the Top

Half of all our best intentions to solve a problem or take advantage of an opportunity in business fail, and the intended outcome of the change or new idea is never realized. And that's an average across all sectors and organization sizes; failure rates of new initiatives in some specific industries are reportedly as high as 90 percent!

The reason why initiatives fail is more surprising than those incredible rates of failure. It's not that the ideas were bad or that change made the plan obsolete. Management's best intentions fail because leaders don't get enough buy-in to power follow-through at every level of the organization.

One of the best ways of gaining buy-in from the rest of the top leaders is by involving them in the creation and drafting of the guiding principles. Committing your guiding principles to paper shouldn't take long. Chances are good that there are already a number of values you share. It shouldn't require more than a couple of hours of discussion and a brief revisit a few days later to formalize their acceptance.

This exercise will also be the perfect opportunity to gauge the attitudes and degree of buy-in from those closest to you. Members of your senior leadership team who pooh-pooh the idea of having and making decisions in accordance with a set of guiding principles aren't worth having around. Internal subversion has irreparably damaged and destroyed more businesses than economic conditions or the rigors of the marketplace. You can't afford to have any senior leaders who fail to see the need for a unifying set of guiding principles and won't be seen as actively supporting them. As Richard Smucker told me, "If we could hire a sales manager tomorrow who could double or triple our revenues but didn't believe in our values, we wouldn't hire them."

Buy-in takes trust, and only a fool trusts those who don't practice what they preach. The best way to begin is to hold up a mirror to the members of the senior leadership team and make certain that in all their actions and decisions they are practicing and living the guiding principles. The saying "Do as I say, not as I do" is a universally demoralizing turnoff.

Flow Guiding Principles Through the Company

In the past decade, I've sat through a thousand speeches by various CEOs, and generally I've been impressed that more and more leaders are getting the importance of the people side of the business.

However, I've never seen a more effective speech than one delivered in 2014 by John Hayes, CEO of $9 billion Ball Corporation, to the firm's top several hundred leaders from around the world.

Hayes took the stage and, for ninety minutes, spoke about the five values of the company. As he talked about uncompromising integrity, being close to the firm's customers, behaving like owners, focusing on attention to detail, and being innovative, you could have heard a pin drop. Hayes is no more a natural slick-tongued orator than you or I, but he spoke with such candor, passion, and authenticity that midway through his speech, I wanted to stand up at the back of the room and shout, "I'm here, John, and I'm coming to work for you!"

If you're leading a small company, the best way to move the guiding principles down through the company is in a series of one-on-one or small-group meetings. In a large enterprise, it's better to opt for a gathering of the top leadership and have the top dog present the guiding principles, as John Hayes did at Ball Corporation. Then you can assign all senior leaders the task of holding individual or small-group meetings to discuss the guiding principles soon after the CEO's speech. If the company's top leadership talks about their guiding principles in every meeting, presentation, and speech they deliver and are seen as living them in everything they do, the principles will become an integral part of the organization's DNA.

Post Them Everywhere

Depending on the year, Koch Industries' $120 billion in annual revenues makes it either the largest or the second-largest privately held company in the world. Based on its nonstop growth, constant acquisitions, and entrances and exits in and out of myriad business categories, the company is one of the most agile and urgent enterprises on the planet.

One of the first things I noticed when spending time on Koch's sprawling campus studying the company and interviewing its owner, Charles Koch, was the absence of much art on the walls. Instead, hanging everywhere were posters and banners proclaiming the company's guiding principles. They were even printed on the coffee cups in the cafeteria.

If it's true that calling someone a horse ten times means they'll start looking for hay, then the same applies to guiding principles. When they're everywhere around people and when they encounter them scores of times throughout their typical workday, it's inevitable they'll eventually sink in.

How many times do people have to see the words "integrity," "compliance," "value creation," "principled entrepreneurship," "customer focus," "knowledge," "change," "humility," "respect," and "fulfillment" on their coffee cups and everywhere their eyes turn before they can recite, believe, and practice them . . . or leave?

Celebrate Them

Every achievement or win accomplished through use of the guiding principles should be celebrated.

Start every staff meeting by singling out someone who scored a win through the use of your guiding principles. Or feature on the front page of your Web site the employee of the month who best exemplifies living your values and putting them into action. Display your guiding principles in the reception area; put up a wall of fame with photos and short stories of those who deserve permanent acknowledgment for embracing the guiding principles.

Celebrate your wins by telling stories. People learn a lot from stories, so institutionalizing storytelling as a vital part of your culture is a great way to ensure that your values are being discussed organically and in the context of real work. Host regular small and large sixty-minute gatherings whose sole purpose is to share stories of the guiding principles and how they've positively impacted the business. Provide small gift cards and restaurant and movie coupons, and let the group vote on the best stories and examples.

As important as celebrating achievements is *not* acknowledging or reveling in an achievement that was realized through behavior out of line with the guiding principles. For example, leaders of a company that celebrates a huge contract win, handsomely rewards the person who got it done, and later pays millions of dollars in fines because bribery was involved had better be very careful about extolling their adherence to high ethical standards, or they will be revealed as thugs. When someone gains a win for your company outside your stated principles, you must never wink and look the other way but instead fire them or tell them that if it ever happens again, they're done.

Put Someone in Charge

Gaylor Electric, based in Indianapolis, Indiana, is a highly successful and rapidly growing electrical contractor with more than two thousand employees and hundreds of millions of dollars in annual revenue. The firm's guiding principles include safety, performance, customer service, teamwork, integrity, personal development, return on investment, and growth. Chuck Goodrich, the executive vice president of the firm, who heads the company's Indiana operations, explains that when it comes to the guiding principles, "Everyone is expected to know them, practice them, and make all their decisions in accordance with them."

But Goodrich has learned that it's not what you say but what you do that gets buy-in. "It's vitally important that every member of the leadership team be seen as doing what we say," he says. And that starts with Goodrich himself.

Goodrich appointed a chief values officer to help him personally stay on track in following the guiding principles. "Every Wednesday morning you'll find me at a local Perkins Restaurant having an early breakfast and spending two hours with our CVO," he says, "going over every decision I've made the previous week and every decision I'm about to make, examining each through the lens of whether or not the decision fits our guiding principles." Perhaps even better would be to have the position of CVO rotate among a wide roster of people ranging from young millennial employees to tribal elders and from the ranks of the workforce to management, with each serving a month on the job.

"We're a great company, committed to speed and growth, and it's easy to accidentally stray out of bounds or be tempted to," Goodrich says, adding, "It's vitally important we have someone making certain that won't happen."

Make Guiding Principles a Big Part of the Hiring Decision

It doesn't make any sense to wait and reveal your guiding principles to a new employee after he or she has been hired. Applicants should be engaged in discussion about your company's values at every stage of the hiring process. Share the guiding principles from the outset, then test applicants on their knowledge of the principles and make certain they are on board with them and understand that all decisions are made in accordance with them. If new hires understand and agree with a company's guiding principles before they join up, the company won't make the mistake of hiring someone who might be a problem from day one.

Get Rid of the CAVE people

Despite your best efforts to help them out, one of the big challenges occasionally faced by leaders is facing card-carrying members of Citizens Against Virtually Everything. These are the whiners, whingers, and complainers who believe that yesterday was better than tomorrow and that the company's best days were in the past. They proudly taunt others with their cynicism, resisting the goodness of any initiative because they see a dark, sinister purpose lurking everywhere. They're not about to get on board with any set of guiding principles and will continually work behind the scenes to derail them. Go ahead and counsel them one more time; try to get them on board. But if you fail, they need to leave. Do it for cause, do it legally, and do it quickly.

A sense of urgency occurs most easily when everyone is constantly cooperating, coordinating, and communicating. The best way to ensure that these things happen is to make certain everyone knows and plays by the same set of rules. Rules, shared by all the members of the community, are how cultures are created.

FAST TASKS

- Make a list of values that you believe should become the guiding principles of the business. Ask a few trusted people from various levels within the organization to do the same.

- Get together with other senior leaders to discuss and build a list of proposed principles using the input you got in step one. Revisit them a few days later and come to agreement on the final list.

- Use the guiding principles of J.M. Smucker as a template for drafting your list. State the principle and then add several lines of text that explain it further and make it come alive.

- Every member of the leadership team should prepare a five-minute speech about the guiding principles of the business and be able to deliver a short elevator-pitch version or longer, more conversational version of it whenever the opportunity arises.

- If yours is a small business, get everyone in the company together to explain the importance of having a set of guiding principles and introduce yours. In a larger enterprise, meet with your direct reports to introduce the principles and develop a plan to move them throughout the organization as quickly as possible.

- Post your guiding principles everywhere.

- Build a plan for constantly communicating and celebrating them.

- Whether you head a small or large business, consider putting someone in charge of protecting and promoting values as a CVO.

- Get rid of the CAVE people.

CHAPTER THREE

The Customer

THE IMMUTABLE LAW OF SUCKAGE

By the time a company recognizes it sucks, it has sucked for a very long time. That's our immutable law of suckage.

Bill Zollars watched the immutable law of suckage destroy a great company. He worked at Kodak for twenty years, hoping to eventually become CEO. Over time he realized that even if he did get the big promotion, there might not be much of a company left to lead after that immutable law trashed it. Kodak refused to adapt to digital and change the conventional film business even as consumers told it, as early as 1981, "Paying to develop a whole roll of film to get just three good pictures sucks." Despite the fact that digital photography (invented by Kodak) was just what customers wanted, executives considered it "the enemy" and "an evil that would kill sales and profits." They fought it tooth and nail until it was too late.

Zollars left to become the CEO of another company, Yellow Freight. He was determined not to allow missteps that he'd seen cripple Kodak be repeated at his new company, so he immediately started searching for any signs of suckage in its customers' minds.

He started by asking his senior leadership team, "What do our clients think of us?"

"Our customers really like us!" they assured him.

His next step was to have the senior leaders personally call about five hundred recent clients, asking them four quick questions about their last experience with the company: Did we pick it up on time? Did we deliver it on time? Did your shipment arrive in good shape, with no scratches, dents, or breakage? Did you get an accurate bill?

Forty percent of the customers said, "Sorry, but the honest answer is no," to one or more of those questions.

Zollars couldn't believe the disastrous truth buried in the survey. How could his senior leadership team be so delusional as to think all the clients liked the company when it had let down four out of ten of them? A little digging revealed the answer. Before Zollars's arrival, Yellow Freight had enlisted a survey company to ask its customers if they were satisfied with the company's performance. Since all the other logistics suppliers the clients dealt with had track records similar to or even worse than Yellow Freight's, most customers said, "I guess so."

The senior leadership team was smart enough to know that truly tough questions (about the fundamental expectations any client has when he or she hires a company like Yellow Freight) hadn't been asked in that survey and that their customers weren't completely satisfied. But that same senior leadership team was unwilling to recognize and implement the changes needed to eliminate customer disappointment. Not much later, on a day that came to be known as Black Friday, Zollars showed most of them the door.

Yellow Freight was spiraling because of the immutable law of suckage. When Zollars's investigation made it clear that 40 percent of customers were genuinely disappointed with Yellow Freight's services, his new team got to work repairing the broken execution of the business fundamentals, boosting the rate of complete satisfaction up to a stellar 96 percent and saving YRC Worldwide (Yellow Freight's parent company), quickly growing it into a $5 billion transportation and logistics company.

We call the law of suckage "immutable" because it happens to companies in all industries. All those top executives in organizations currently circling the bowl, and the ones that have already gone down the drain, failed to see that their companies sucked before they started massively hemorrhaging customers and their suckage soured their remaining client relationships. Why didn't top bosses at Sears, Sony, Sprint, Circuit City, BlackBerry, and Borders recognize the early warning signs and take urgent action instead of lollygagging until massive customer defections made it obvious that they stank to high heaven? It's a question I'm going to help you answer before the law of suckage destroys your chances to grow fast and maintain a high-speed company.

Topping the list of guiding principles at companies with cultures of urgency and growth is the critical importance of anticipating and then exceeding customers' expectations. Whatever a client expects *must* be delivered, and when it's not, that has to be noticed and resolved with absolute urgency.

How Is Your Company Doing?

When some survey monkey calls you and asks, "How satisfied were you on a scale of one to five with X company?" I bet you generally provide a rating of four or five. In doing so, you're basically saying,

"You're pretty much like everybody else." You know if you give them a lower number, they'll likely use it as an excuse to yell at the people who actually tried to help you or they'll send you some ridiculously empty gesture, like a $5 gift card for your next purchase.

In Frederick Reichheld's landmark book *The Loyalty Effect* and all his subsequent research, he reveals that 90 percent of customers who defect from a company actually report they are satisfied with that company's performance. It's probably a fair guess that 90 percent of all customers who stop doing business with you would say they're satisfied with your company's performance as well.

"That just proves to me that all loyalty is dead" is the typical reaction I receive when I bring up the reasons why satisfied customers leave.

Not so fast. More research by Dr. Earl Sasser, a professor at Harvard Business School and the coauthor of the book *The Service Profit Chain* and the influential *Harvard Business Review* article "Why Satisfied Customers Defect," proves that *completely* satisfied customers are six times more likely to become loyal customers. Today's customers aren't any less loyal; they just have fewer barriers stopping them from defecting when you disappoint them. Complete satisfaction still keeps and grows your customer base.

The reason for a culture of urgency is to grow your business revenues and improve your financial performance, allowing you to get closer to fulfilling your purpose. You can't pull that off without finding, keeping, and growing the right customers and making certain you don't fall victim to the immutable law of suckage. You need to get close to the customers, discover how they live their lives, and learn their hopes, needs, wants, aspirations, and dreams. Only then can you have the understanding and the motivation to exceed your customers' expectations and totally satisfy them. Before you say, "We're too big and too busy for all that 'close to the customer' stuff," you need to read how they do it at the $85 billion giant Procter & Gamble.

A High-Speed Company Really Knows Its Customers

As a researcher, I really respect Procter & Gamble. It's endured for almost 180 years with lifetime revenues in the trillions and profits adding up to hundreds of billions, and it has big plans for the future: a goal of adding six hundred million new customers and creating an astonishing five billion loyal Procter & Gamble households worldwide.

P&G has nailed everything covered in the first two chapters. The company does well by doing good and has the magic words to prove it: "We create and build brands that improve consumers' lives." The company has a set of guiding principles (which includes eliminating organizational barriers that get in the way of growth, treating the company's assets as you would your own, always being honest and straightforward, having a passion for winning, and being externally focused) by which all decisions are made.

Most important, I respect P&G because it has beaten the curse of the big, the old, and the successful. Having invested many years doing postmortems on business behemoths, I've found most to be brittle, stiff, and resistant to change. Without exception, they are also all painfully slow to adapt. Not P&G; it flexes and bends like a yoga instructor. Its leaders are curious, open, and imaginative like the best entrepreneurs. And the company routinely surprises critics with its fast thinking and urgency.

How does Procter & Gamble keep its organization fresh and fast to beat the immutable law of suckage? I found the answer, perhaps surprisingly, in Istanbul.

In 2013 I was hired to give a keynote speech about leadership and growth in Turkey to a group of the top worldwide leaders of Procter & Gamble's Fabric Care division. Fabric Care (think Tide, Ariel, and Downy) is huge for P&G, bringing in more than $17 billion annually. P&G also offered me an opportunity to play a role on a few "home visits," something not normally afforded to outsiders.

The thousands of off-site conferences that P&G holds for the 130,000 members of its global workforce each year look a lot like the conferences you're used to attending. Big hotel conference rooms nicely staged, great food, plenty of fellowship, and lots of business to discuss. The difference is that P&G takes care of conference business between seven thirty and noon and then, instead of golf, spa visits, or team-building whitewater-rafting excursions, attendees always spend the afternoon calling on prospects and customers.

All of them, including executives up to the president and CEO, line up outside the hotel in teams of two to be picked up and driven to their destinations. Half the teams visit the stores and retailers that sell their packaged goods and the other half visit consumers in their homes. I was paired with Fabric Care's Switzerland-based female VP of marketing to go on a home visit.

The company's Turkish research contractor had lined up hundreds of families who, in return for a gift bag including restaurant and movie coupons and free merchandise at local stores, would welcome us (and our interpreters) into their homes for a two-hour conversation. The families were told only that the visit was by a company doing research.

Our first trip was to the home of a middle-class Turkish family earning about $1,000 monthly. The father worked as a barber, so we were told we would be spending time with his wife, the mother of two female preteens.

After climbing several flights of stairs in a very old, traditional

Turkish building, we were welcomed warmly into a five-room apartment, where we removed our shoes and were seated in the family's living room. They were a traditional Muslim family, so it took some adjustment to figure out the appropriate setup to accommodate my presence, as a Western, non-Muslim man.

There were two translators, one asking in Turkish the questions we told her to ask and another speaking softly, simultaneously translating into English the questions and answers for us. I was wondering how fast we'd get around to discussing washing detergents, but our list of questions didn't have any specific questions about Tide, Downy, or Ariel. All the questions were about the family—their stories, backgrounds, hopes, and dreams.

After an hour the mother excused herself for a few minutes. The two daughters kept sneaking looks at me and giggling with each other. Soon their mother returned with a huge tray of homemade pastries and carafes of tea and soft drinks. Tears were shed as the mom shared stories and promises about the better lives her girls would have. I couldn't believe how freely this family was discussing the most sensitive of family matters and how much we were learning about them as people.

Finally, toward the end of our planned two-hour visit, the P&G VP began asking a few questions about laundry. The mother invited us to follow her to her combination master bathroom/laundry room, where she showed us her modern automatic washing machine and dryer. On top of the machine was a box of Ariel, a competitor's brand, and a free store sample of another detergent. I was itching to ask her a few questions about her favorite products, loyalties, and willingness to try new brands. Luckily, I held back. If I had barged into all my brand-centric questions then, we would have missed the most valuable piece of information gathered that day.

"I love my washing machine and dryer," she said proudly, "and

I do all the household linens and bedding in them as well the clothing for my husband and me."

"What about the girls' laundry?" I asked.

She looked at me with a horrified expression. "I would never do my daughters' clothing in an automatic washing machine," she exclaimed, "and no other good Turkish mother would. I wash all my daughters' clothing by hand because if my daughters are going to achieve success in school and life, their clothing must be perfect."

Her statement was worth more than a nugget of gold. As odd as it may seem to a westerner, she believed machine washing was not good enough for her children. Hand washing their laundry was a badge of motherly honor to her, just as we might feel about reading a story to our kids rather than turning on the TV.

Although I knew very little about the private inner workings of P&G, I did know it was in the early stages of rolling out a new product in Turkey: detergent pods that you simply drop in a washing machine. I'd be willing to bet there are a few hotshot marketers at the company who have argued that the future of international fabric care is wrapped up in these new pods and that they'd be a perfect answer for every article of clothing including children's wear. While there are probably many early adopters among Turkey's twenty million families willing to try Ariel in pod form, I'd also bet that P&G will be selling powders and liquids (suitable for hand washing) there for a long time, thanks to the insights gained through the in-person visits it conducted. By staying close to consumers through hundreds of thousands of in-home interviews, in every country where it does business, and hearing and seeing firsthand where its customers live, how they live, and their hopes for the future, P&G is able to completely satisfy their wants and needs and avoid the pitfalls of the immutable law of suckage.

By late afternoon, all the teams had completed their home visits and everyone gathered again in the hotel ballroom. One by one, the teams took the stage and reported what they had encountered on their home visits. The only condition was that every team had to share their experiences in the form of a narrative or story: no analytics, no numbers, just stories, complete with pictures taken on smartphones.

I sat, riveted, for hours as the teams presented one remarkable insight after another. My mind was in wild overdrive—like, four Red Bulls' worth—as one big question pinged around in my head: Why doesn't every company, no matter its size, copy P&G's home visits?

Is it because they don't care enough about their customers? Are they so arrogant as to believe they already know what customers are thinking? Are they relying on the same type of irrelevant data so many companies receive from their research companies, telling them that their customers are satisfied? Did they tell themselves it would cost too much money to do the same thing? Or did nobody show them how to do it?

The answer to the first four questions is yes. Here's why.

Don't Row, Row, Row *That* Boat

"We've got a rowboat mentality," said the former chairman and CEO of Sony, Howard Stringer. He meant that while leaders were working to power the business forward, they mistakenly had their eyes glued on where they'd been. Sony's television division, the technology and quality leader, has lost $10 billion in the last decade, partly due to management's looking backward and not anticipating the future.

There's a valid reason managers focus heavily on where they've been. All the guidance they get is from the numbers on a profit and loss statement. P&L numbers are valuable; they are straight talk for leaders: clear, specific, and unemotional. But those numbers can show you only where you've been. They don't anticipate what's ahead and almost never call out trouble looming on the horizon.

In the late 1990s I researched the challenges facing the media industry (television, radio, and newspapers) in the twenty-first century for several industry trade associations. I learned a stunning fact that was buried in their client research: 47 percent of new advertising clients didn't come back to buy again because results, in their minds, sucked.

"Your business bucket has a gaping hole in it," I told these trade associations. "Almost half of your new clients don't come back a second time. That's trouble." If new clients thought the results sucked, I reasoned, old clients were likely feeling dissatisfied as well.

"But our revenues are ahead of last year," they said, using that view from the rowboat. True. That's because they were adding more customers than were defecting.

"Ultimately," the media bosses said in confidence, "what are these businesses going to do? We're the only game in town." That was also true at the time; the first banner ad didn't appear until 1994, and Google didn't even exist until 1998. So they sat on their hands, doing nothing substantial to address their clients' disappointment.

Today that rowboat mentality and the immutable law of suckage have caught up with the media industry. From 2003 to 2013, newspaper ad revenues fell from $44.9 billion to $18.9 billion. And despite everything you read in those papers, it wasn't primarily the invention of online advertising that slowed revenues and caused profits to fall again and again. The companies just refused to acknowledge that they sucked, even though their clients had felt they sucked for a long, long time.

Looking only backward, keeping your eyes on where you've been, won't do anything to help you build a high-speed company committed to growing as fast as possible.

Nothing Fails Like Success

A wise man said, "Those the gods wish to destroy they first call 'promising.'"

- One of the promising companies of my youth was Kmart. In 1976 it had 1,206 big stores in the United States. Walmart had 125. Today, by comparison, Kmart gets smaller and smaller every year, its revenues go down each year, and Walmart owns retail with a half trillion dollars in annual revenues.

- Another promising company was the Gap (actually composed of the Gap, Old Navy, and the Banana Republic), which exploded from $1.9 billion in sales in 1990 to $15 billion by 2009. Then the Gap got stuck. First, Spanish retailer Zara zoomed past it, and then Sweden's H&M, with 3,200 stores and 116,000 employees, brought in revenue of $23 billion, leaving the Gap in the dust.

- In 1988 one in four beers sold in America was a Budweiser. By 2011 it was just one in twelve. Yet the company keeps trotting out the Clydesdales, sleigh bells, and gently falling snow in its television commercials as though everything were hunky-dory.

Success is a double-edged sword. It's exactly what we need to invest in our future. But success can turn risk takers into caretakers, holding on to processes and tactics long after those processes and tactics stop adding value. Many successful managers become more preoccupied with internal issues and more paranoid about satisfying the hierarchy than concerned with exceeding the expectations of the customers.

Success also brings with it an army of yes-men who think their job is to filter everything the owner or CEO sees and hears. Leaders get badly distorted pictures of the state of the business, the dissatisfaction of customers, and the need for change because of these yes-men. When Bain & Company surveyed 362 top executives and asked if their company delivered a superior performance to their customers, 80 percent said, "Yes!" But when they asked the customers of those same companies to evaluate their work, 92 percent said, "Superior performance? I don't think so!" How could those CEOs be so clueless? Because an army of yes-men shields bosses from any brutal facts.

CREATING AND CASCADING "CUSTOMERS FIRST"

The night of my P&G home-visit experience in Istanbul, I was tossing and turning in bed, replaying scenes of the day: the excited anticipation of the P&Gers eager to make their visits and the scores of insights and observations shared by the presenters back at the hotel. Most of all I thought about the rare opportunity I'd had to spend the day with people who truly cared about the people with whom they did business.

When A. G. Lafley rejoined P&G in 2013 as the company's chairman, CEO, and president, he sent a message to every employee that said, "Going forward, let's remember our customer is boss!"

How do you, like Lafley, stay ahead of the immutable law of suckage and stay tuned to your customer in order to keep your company nimble?

Know the Value of Your Customers

In order to think fast and move faster and grow the business, you need to do a checkup from the neck up. Negative attitudes, biases, overconfidence, and resistance to change cause more stalls in business than any recession.

Your checkup starts with understanding the immense value of a regular customer.

- Starbucks knows that its average customer is worth just under $300 a year. What is your *average* customer worth each year?

- United Airlines knows 9 percent of its clients generate 46 percent of the total revenue. What are your *best* customers worth each year?

The average pay TV subscriber will spend about $40,000 over his or her lifetime. What will your *average* customer spend in a lifetime?

Here's an easy formula for determining the value of customer:

Average value of a transaction

x Average number of repeat transactions annually

x Years of average (or potential) retention rate

= Lifetime value of the customer

Let's look at this formula in a restaurant where the average ticket is $50 for two people. If the average customer dines there once weekly and the potential retention rate is ten years, the potential lifetime value of a customer is a whopping $26,000. Are you treated as though you're about to spend $26,000 when you walk into most restaurants? I'm not!

Now let's apply the same formula for a trainer in a gym. The trainer charges $80 a session, sees his average client twice weekly, and has the potential to keep the right customer for ten years or more. The potential lifetime value of his customer is an astounding $83,000 plus.

Any business can generate sufficient data to determine the annual and lifetime value of a good customer. Doing the math and training everyone in the company to imagine every potential customer with his potential lifetime spend written on a Post-it note on his forehead is a good starting point.

Implement a Listening Program

Follow the lead of P&G and set up a program for regularly talking with and listening to customers and prospective customers. The program will depend on the size of your business and the resources available, but no organization will ever become a high-speed company without having an institutionalized program of listening to the marketplace.

The best advice for setting up such a program is what I learned living at our lake house during the summer. Sometimes ice doesn't melt on our lake in far-northern Michigan until the middle of May, which means that in June, when people start moving into their cabins and lodges for the summer, the water is still very cold. Each year, as I take my kayak for the first spin around the lake, I observe the torturous ritual of people standing on their docks, about to take the first jump of summer into the water. Shouts of "You go first!" are answered with an equally loud "No, *you* go first!" Back and forth the taunting continues for a long time, until finally one brave soul steps forward and takes the first plunge. Predictably, everyone else follows.

You—the leader—have to take the plunge first, jump in, and spearhead the creation of a program for listening to your customers and prospective customers. You are responsible for understanding the importance of keeping your company's collective finger on the pulse of the marketplace so the law of suckage doesn't bring the whole enterprise down.

Set the wheels in motion by scheduling five one-hour visits with existing customers and another five with potential customers within a five-day time period. Letting it become widely known within the company that you're spending the bulk of a week out listening to customers will send a powerful message to your organization about your priorities and value. (In chapter 6 you'll learn more about the kinds of questions you should ask in these types of meetings.)

I have literally brought groups of highly accomplished C-suite leaders to sleepless nights, anxiety attacks, and teary eyes when I've assigned them this task—and believe me, I've heard every possible excuse for not doing it. "I'm too busy," "I have people who do this for me," "I have more important things to do" . . . On and on the excuses have gone. The seat in the office is more comfortable but the seat in the car is always more profitable. Take the plunge and jump in first. I also promise you that once you've jumped in, everyone else will want to emulate you and do the same.

These ten visits, done alone by you, will teach you more about your company, your customers, and the changes you need to make than the terabytes of raw customer data you might have and, by the end of the week, the program that you need to create will become obvious.

There is no friggin' excuse for not doing this now!

Learn to Say You're Sorry and Show You Mean It

High-speed companies with an authentic purpose of doing something good and a solid set of guiding principles get in less trouble and do fewer stupid things than other companies, but once in a while something can go wrong for them too, and they'll need to apologize to a customer or customers. In 2013 trendy yoga-wear company Lululemon got into hot water when complaints came to light about its yoga pants being "too sheer." Lululemon's cofounder and chairman Chip Wilson said that the reason the pants were too sheer was because "they don't work for certain women's bodies." Yikes! He was heard by women everywhere to be saying, "You might be too fat to wear our pants."

When he apologized for those comments, the apology was as tone-deaf as the original offense. Speaking by video to employees (and not customers), Wilson said, "I'm sad for the repercussions of my actions. . . . I take responsibility. . . . I ask you [employees] to stay in the conversation that is above the fray." That's not how you say you're sorry! Wilson stepped down a few months later, but the damage to the company was already done; Lululemon's share price had fallen 44 percent as of August 2014.

Bob Engel of CoBank found himself doing a lot of apologizing when he came in as president and COO. "I spent much of my first four years falling on my sword, apologizing for some terrible behavior and trying to rebuild credibility. I apologized so often, sometimes I wasn't sure what I was apologizing for," he says. "I had to go to customers one by one to convince them that we were going to be different from now on." CoBank and some of its predecessors had behaved poorly, like a lot of banks; according to Engel, "When the times got tough we said, the way bankers do, 'See you later.' Customers couldn't count on us in the tough times to treat them right."

If you want to avoid defections and recover from outrage and regret your company created when you failed to deliver what was expected, Engel says you've got to learn to say you're sorry for a misstep and show you mean it. Here's his advice:

- Use your "A" team.

You can't outsource your recovery process to a call center or your newest low level associates. You need the coolest, most strategic-minded executives who are marvelous communicators. You need someone who thinks like the owner, who loves the customer, and who has his or her heart in the right place.

"I've always believed the toughest jobs belong to the CEO," Engel says. "Let me and my top people deal with the harder stuff. We've got the stripes (the authority) to convince someone when we say it's going to be different, it will be."

- Listen, really listen.

You need to understand, not be understood. That means listening with your full attention to your customers, getting the full story, feeling the weight of their disappointment, wearing your heart on your sleeve, and pressing them for all the ugly details until they say, "That's everything." The best outcome is to reach the point where they say, "Maybe I've gone a bit too far. Thanks for hearing me out."

Engel remembers a time one of his customers read him the riot act in public during a conference. "He jabbed his finger at me and said, 'When we hit a wall, you guys turned the knob on us, made our lives miserable, and didn't care a bit!'" Engel recalls. "'CoBank is a swear word in our offices now. It's cussing just to say your name.' Man, he really let me have it. I was there in front of a huge crowd of other Florida cooperative agribusiness customers, and I knew I had to just take it. It felt like he went on for an eternity but I bit my lip and didn't interrupt. When he was done, I said, 'I feel terrible. You're right and we were absolutely wrong. No one should treat customers like that. Give me a chance. I'm going to get this fixed.' We did, and now he's a big customer and one of my best friends."

- Don't jump to resolutions.

The executive who jumps to a resolution spoils all the goodwill and trust she achieved through patient listening. "When you hurry to make an offer it's as if you're saying, 'I was thinking about something else while you were talking. How about we give you a voucher? Would that make you happy?'" Engel explains.

Engel took the time to consider all the facts, measure the lifetime value of a good customer, and consider how he'd feel if he were in the customer's shoes. "Give yourself a good talking to," he says. "Then you can make your decision."

- Take heavy action.

"This is about as painful as it gets for a guy like me," Engel says sadly. "But I have to tell you the story.

"A few years ago, we learned that some of our people [at Co-Bank] had crossed an ethical line in terms of getting market information about one of our competitors. Legally, I can't go into details, but their actions were clearly not in keeping with our corporate values or standards of professional conduct. Once their behavior had come to light, we took heavy action inside the company.

We came clean with the board and our bank regulators, and some otherwise good people ended up leaving CoBank. We instituted a new ethics training and compliance program and hired a chief ethics officer, who answers to the board directly."

Engel didn't stop there. "CoBank took a step that many considered unnecessary—we settled with the competitor within a few months." He also asked the board to claw back a portion of his own incentive bonus for the period.

"Ultimately, I'm the one responsible," he told them. "And no one will know we're seriously sorry unless we take heavy action. A bad experience weighs five times as much as a good one. So to get someone back to equilibrium, you can't be stingy. You've got to be substantial. You need heavy action."

A great apology should make your accountant or your lawyers think, *Is that really necessary?*

Push Yourself to Anticipate Disappointment

Imagine trying your luck at Harrah's Las Vegas. After a couple of hours watching your pile of chips shrink, it crosses your mind that gaming at Harrah's is more pain than gain.

But just before you reach the end of your rope, an executive comes over and says, "Hi. I noticed you're having a bit of a rough patch. I know how that feels. You've enjoyed dinner at Ruth's Chris Steak House in the past, right? How about you and your wife have dinner right now, my treat?"

Caesars Entertainment Total Rewards loyalty cards do more than deliver special offers and points to redeem. As Ian Ayres explains in *Super Crunchers,* Total Rewards helps management anticipate the "pain point" for guests, alerting them to how much a player can lose and still enjoy the experience enough to keep coming back. For some customers it's $900. For others it's much higher. When the database senses a gambler is nearing his predicted pain point, a Harrah's "luck ambassador" is dispatched to fix the situation before it reaches the breaking point. It's vitally important to anticipate customers' pain points.

No organization achieves perfection. The next best thing is to nip disappointment in the bud through anticipating pain points and taking the initiative.

Ban That Other *F* Word

"Twenty years ago you waited in a line, left your car for days, and when we called to say it's ready, you were thankful," an exasperated auto executive told me. "Now we do warranty work while you wait and built a plush lounge to keep everyone entertained. We do pickup and drop-off. We give people a loaner car. Our techs have better bedside manners than the Mayo Clinic. We're even detailing your car when we're done for free. I've spent a million dollars on my customers in the last five years and still they want more. When will it end?"

Like the little kid who keeps pestering from the backseat with "Are we there yet?" business has too many people who are always wondering, "Are we finished yet?"

No business that hopes to keep thinking fast and moving faster will ever be finished when it comes to completely satisfying its customers. As expectations are met, customers want more. People's priorities change, they want something new, and they want you to realize it without their having to tell you. You can never shift focus to other matters. You are *never* finished combating suckage.

Mike Long, the CEO of Arrow Electronics, has built his

company into a $25 billion powerhouse with eighteen thousand employees, serving more than one hundred thousand OEMs (original equipment manufacturers) from five hundred locations in sixty countries. Long says, "When you know the value of a customer, and everyone in your company, from the bottom to the top, hangs out with customers, constantly asking, 'What else itches that we can scratch?' 'What's causing you pain that we make go away?' and 'What else can we do to help you get to where you want to go?' you realize you're never finished; you're just getting started and everything has to be approached with urgency."

Customers are the only asset any company possesses, and their being completely satisfied is the lifeblood of longevity. Companies that successfully compete in a nanosecond culture understand that efforts to replace customers who are leaving as fast as they're being added is a waste of time. Truly high-speed companies don't let the immutable law of suckage put them in that position.

FAST TASKS

- Make ten visits to customers and prospective customers, as prescribed in the chapter. Dress casually, don't record the meetings, and spend most of the time asking customers questions about themselves and their needs. If you're a B2B company, talk about their business, not yours. Make your notes after you've left the meeting.

- After your ten visits, schedule a meeting with your key people, your direct reports, or, in the case of a very small business, your staff, and spend an hour telling stories about what you've learned. At the end of the meeting, assign them the same task, to be completed within a week. Follow up after their visit, and listen to them relay stories of their listening assignments.

- When you've completed these Fast Tasks, you will have learned so much about your customers that you will create a program of ongoing listening. I'd love to hear what form yours takes.

CHAPTER FOUR

Transparency

MORE TRUST, MORE ENGAGEMENT, MORE URGENCY

Urgency comes from having a thoroughly engaged workforce—disengaged people don't think or act fast. Pulling together an engaged workforce, however, is a huge challenge.

Current studies and surveys expose the facts that employees have never been more disconnected and cynical and that overall trust in business has fallen to an all-time low. According to the 2014 Edelman Trust Barometer, only one in five people believes business leaders tell the truth and make ethical and moral decisions.

This trend won't be reversed anytime soon. There are approximately one hundred million millennials (those born between 1980 and the early 2000s), who will make up the bulk of your workforce in the years to come. If you haven't already noticed, millennials are a tough crowd. The 2012 University of Chicago General Social

Survey shows that only 19 percent of millennials think that most people can be trusted. Good luck using the standard carrot-and-stick incentives and the justification that "That's the way things have always been done" to get them engaged in your efforts to be fast.

Because employees across demographics tend to distrust business and business leaders, they're less likely to quickly adopt new thinking and follow through on new ideas. In 2008 I learned of a study designed to assess the range of cooperative behavior between people that was conducted by Dr. Robert Kurzban of the University of Pennsylvania and Dr. Daniel Houser of George Mason University. The scholars concluded that 83 percent of people just sit on their hands at the beginning of the implementation of any new idea. Only 17 percent will pitch in immediately.

I've shared those conclusions from Kurzban and Houser with executives for six years now, and every manager admits to having seen this firsthand at his or her own company. Many senior leaders have shared personal stories of the insurmountable inertia they face whenever they ask teams to embrace change.

However, there's a silver lining in those gloomy numbers. Only 20 percent of people will *never* agree to pitch in and help implement a new initiative or change in routine; they're called the "free riders" by academics. Sixty-three percent of people who are sitting on their hands at the beginning of a new initiative—the overwhelming majority—can be persuaded to get on board and do their part if they can *trust* that it's safe to get involved and that there's a good chance of success. Give them that, and they'll get to their feet quickly, ready and willing to follow through. What this proves is that only when you find a way to gain people's trust and get more buy-in can speed become your competitive advantage.

No business executive, owner, or CEO has ever done a better job of figuring out how to gain people's trust, rid them of their cynicism, and get them to think and move fast than the man you're about to meet. His key to buy-in was taking *transparency* to a whole new level.

Transparency on Steroids

It all started with one very gutsy move.

Jack Stack was thirty-three and had moved himself up from mailroom worker to plant superintendent when International Harvester sent him to Springfield, Missouri, to fix one of the company's ailing manufacturing plants. He arrived to find the plant losing money and teetering on the edge of bankruptcy. Putting his midwestern work ethic into overdrive, Stack rolled up his sleeves and went to work fixing the business.

It didn't take Stack long to realize that Harvester had bigger problems than just this one business unit in Springfield. In the spirit of being open and transparent, he called his managers together and laid the situation out for them. "One of three things is going to happen to us, despite anything we accomplish here in Springfield," he told them. "Harvester will either sell us, shut us down, or we'll all die a slow death while they cut us off from any fresh capital investment."

Seeing the roomful of crestfallen faces, Stack recognized there was a fourth possibility, as outlandish as it seemed. All the managers at the plant could get together to buy the company from Harvester and save it themselves. As Stack rolled the idea around in his head, he concluded that, far-fetched or not, he had no alternative but to try it.

He traveled to Harvester's headquarters and broached the idea of buying the company. Eager to rid itself of a money-losing plant, the company named a price of $9 million. At the time, Stack had a liquid net worth of just $30,000. His other twelve managers were able to scrape together an additional $70,000.

While conventional wisdom doesn't allow for purchasing a $9 million asset with essentially a 1.1 percent down payment, nobody had told Jack Stack that. He earnestly began pitching bankers and other investors, asking them to invest the remaining $8.9 million. After two years of hard slogging, a lot of runarounds, much eye rolling, and even more "noes," a group of individual investors finally said yes and Stack got his money at a credit-card interest rate of 18 percent. He had $100,000 in equity and eighty-nine times that in debt. But leveraging his new company to the hilt was not the craziest thing he did in his pursuit of this new company.

The twenty-four-month saga of talking to bankers and other possible investors had forced Jack Stack to learn something new and important: Finance 101. He learned to compute equity and liquidity ratios, debt and bond financing, cash flow, gross margin, return on investment, and how to read every single line of a P&L and balance sheet. He learned the vital signs of a business; because of this, he also knew he'd put his company at the very edge of a steep and deadly cliff. This didn't deter him, though. If anything, Stack was excited because he understood what it would take to make the plant a financial success. He reasoned that if he shared that information with all the company's employees, if they had all the knowledge he had and understood everyone's part in creating success, people would do the right thing for the business.

Then Stack made his gutsiest move ever: He opened the books to the entire company and taught every team member, at every level, how to read and understand each line of every critical financial report—profit and loss statement, cash flow and receivables, key ratios, how the numbers were all interrelated—and, most important, what each employee could do to improve the numbers. He called his new system the "Great Game of Business." It was transparency on steroids.

Businesses have talked for years about getting everyone to think like the owner and take charge of his or her business unit. Some have even posted versions of tightly redacted accounting reports. But only a handful have ever opened the books to their company's entire staff. Jack Stack was certainly among the first to actually teach his people what every number meant and how employee actions at every level, all the way to the top, affected those numbers.

His big gamble paid off. Today SRC Holdings has thirty-eight companies employing 1,400 owners, does $550 million in annual revenues, and creates and opens two new businesses every year. The average employee will retire from SRC with shares worth about $600,000 (though some have left with as much as $25 million), and the company's stock valuation, which was ten cents a share when Stack and his managers bought the company, has been as high as $200 a share.

Transparency has stuck. Once a week, at all of SRC's thirty-eight companies, the entire workforce reports to the lunchroom to review reports on cash, sales, profits, the business pipeline, and the key ratios that make a business successful. And it's not just that Jack Stack's SRC Holdings is transparent—it's that the transparency gets the entire team on the same page about what their culture is and how it operates and allows them to act quickly and decisively when they need to.

CREATING AND CASCADING TRANSPARENCY

Jack Stack made big moves to create a culture of transparency. Every CEO, company owner, or head of a start-up should do the same. As Stack's company's performance made clear, there's no better way to destroy cynicism and gain trust than by opening up the books, making sure everyone knows how they can be a player in the great game of business, and sharing the wealth with those who create it.

For a variety of reasons, however, "open the books and teach people all the numbers" may not be possible for you. Perhaps you run a department, not a whole company, and are not in a position to open and teach the books. That's okay . . . for now. You don't have to start with complete disclosure of all your company's numbers to gain back a lot of trust lost by previous bosses and society in general. Here are the steps you can take toward greater transparency and destruction of cynicism, things you can do that will make a huge impact by fostering openness among your team.

Connect the Dots

Everyone who works for you should know how their role creates value for the company. They should especially learn the economic value they create and how it can be measured (by you and them). Stack's example shows that connecting those dots increases everyone's engagement and contribution.

Some argue that it's not possible to figure out the economic value created by an assistant, a receptionist, or someone working in IT or HR. That's simply not true and little more than a bad excuse for not doing the hard work necessary to creatively think about such metrics.

SSM Health Care (the remarkable group of twenty large acute-care hospitals and 150 outpatient sites you read about in chapter 1) figured it out. It began connecting the dots by defining the five characteristics that would distinguish an "exceptional" health care provider from the average. Those five characteristics were exceptional clinical outcomes, exceptional patient satisfaction, exceptional employee satisfaction, exceptional physician/partner satisfaction, and exceptional financial results.

Next SSM set a yardstick for each of those five "exceptionals." For example, lowering rates for unplanned readmittance to well below the national average would make a hospital's clinical outcomes exceptional; and faster response to requests for pain management would earn it exceptional scores in patient satisfaction. Once this was established, the leadership team at SSM detailed each of the five exceptionals so that every employee could see what his or her unit had to do to contribute to making the company successful.

Finally, leadership and line supervisors connected the dots by requesting that every department set goals for improvement on each of the exceptional factors and track its progress in increasing them. By the time they were done, each and every employee knew if and how he or she was adding value to the organization by the end of every shift.

Stop All the "Closed Door" Nonsense

I first met Cliff Hudson, the chairman and CEO of Sonic Corp., when I showed up at the company's Oklahoma City headquarters to spend a day with him. He's the person responsible for quickly growing the company from 1,500 to 3,600 locations and maintaining Sonic as one of only ten American companies to have grown revenues and profits by double digits for fifteen consecutive years.

One of my researchers and I came to the third-floor reception desk, announced ourselves to the person manning the desk, and asked if he could direct us to Mr. Hudson's office. The man smiled and said, "Well, I'm Mr. Hudson, but people call me Cliff and *this* is my office."

"The reception desk is your office?" I asked incredulously.

"A couple years ago the receptionist went on maternity leave and I decided to move out to her desk for a week or so to see what it would be like," he said. "I liked it so much that I never went back to having a private office."

"What about when you have to talk about important stuff that has to stay private or secret?" I asked.

"When publicly traded companies have to go behind closed doors and talk about secret stuff," he said, "they're probably going to do something really stupid and get in loads of trouble. We don't have any secrets here!"

Contrast Cliff Hudson's attitude toward secrecy with what I recently witnessed at a large health insurance company's meeting in Chicago. I was scheduled to give the opening speech to their top three hundred people. Coffee and registration were at 7:30 a.m.; the event was due to start an hour later with a short welcome by the CEO before my keynote.

I showed up early, rehearsed, and spent an hour shaking hands and introducing myself to the attendees. Promptly at 8:25, a hotel worker with meeting chimes began walking through the crowd to let everyone know the session was about to begin. As I started to head into the ballroom, a woman grabbed my arm and asked, "Where are you going?"

"Into the ballroom," I said. "I'm Jason Jennings, the guy doing the speech."

"I know who you are, but you're not allowed in there," she said rather sternly.

"Well, how in the world am I going to deliver a speech to your group if I'm not allowed in there?" I asked.

"You can't be in there while the CEO is welcoming people to the event," she said, with a great deal of self-importance in her voice.

"What in the heck are you talking about?" I asked.

"Well," she said, "during his couple of minutes, the CEO might accidentally say something about or inadvertently refer to part of our strategy, and unless you've signed a nondisclosure agreement, you can't be in there. It's all secret."

It was ridiculous. I'd spent hours meeting with the CEO and his top leaders, all of whom had shared with me every element of the company's strategy so I could be a more effective teacher, but this swashbuckling assistant had obviously been told by another one of the self-important secret keepers to not let anyone in.

In most instances, policies like keeping secrets, operating with a "need to know" mentality, and asking people to sign nondisclosure agreements have gone over the top and exist only to confer special status on a few, to let them feel more special than the people they lead. This practice perpetuates the hierarchical BS machine the company has built. Such people's secrets, not their accomplishments, are the only things that allow them to feel important. You can't have transparency when paranoia is an integral part of the culture and everything's hush-hush. In the case of the health insurance company, the *secret keeping* was a symptom of deep cultural problems that continue to cause the company to lag behind all its competitors in urgency and growth.

Telling trade secrets outside the company should get someone's head lopped off, sure. But internal transparency and a shared sense of urgency won't exist in an organization that hoards critical knowledge and tells its employees they can't be trusted.

Make Every Directive Clear

A well-known CEO had impeccable credentials for strategic execution and even wrote a popular book on the subject. Yet when his own division chiefs submitted their strategic plans and budgets for the upcoming fiscal year, he sent them some head-scratching feedback. "What you've got here is good," he wrote, "but to make it better I have some suggestions. First, we need an ambitious plan for productivity that overachieves. Next, our quality problems are disturbing. Continue your work to improve. Three, cost reduction is a big opportunity. One point of cost will take you from an uncomfortable position to a comfortable one." His list went on like that for seventeen similarly phrased bullet points.

What did he mean by an "ambitious plan"? Did he mean a 1 percent, 5 percent, or 25 percent improvement in productivity? Is cost reduction the top priority for next year or somewhere in the middle? Should those "disturbing" quality problems trump cost cutting if the two are in conflict? You don't have any idea, do you? Neither did I when I read it.

Everywhere I go, people say their bosses' directives are not clear and are sometimes in conflict with other directives. They think the reason for all this gobbledygook from headquarters is bosses trying to hide that they don't know what they want, don't know how it should get done, or are nervous about being held accountable for their instructions. Instead they give vague, general, ambiguous direction wrapped in buzzwords and then look annoyed when anyone asks them to clarify.

Transparency starts with clarity. A great step toward transparency in any organization is to say, "I don't know," when you don't know. Ask your team or fellow leaders for help or feedback. If you need time to formulate clarity of strategy, say so! Say, "Let me get the facts and make a decision and get back to you with the answer," instead of trying to buffalo everyone when you don't have a clear directive to give. Then invest the time to come up with clear, specific, prioritized, and conflict-free expectations for your team. Once you establish that level of clarity in direction, especially if your team has seen you do the hard work to really make your directives clear, you can watch their trust soar.

Keep It Simple

Physicist Michio Kaku believes that scientists must keep everything simple. He recommends that his peers accept Einstein's directive: "If you can't explain a theory to a child, it is probably worthless." That's good advice for everyone in business too.

Businesspeople often use jargon, affectations, pseudoeducated buzzwords, and convoluted sentences that obscure rather than explain. Look at what an MBA wrote when he was applying for a new position at his company: "I possess a comprehensive understanding of team development and individual enfranchisement, incremental planning, and crisis accountability while promoting forward-thinking solutions in meeting desired objectives." I'll bet you've seen plenty of similar stuff in strategic plans and policy manuals over the years. Again, it's self-important garbage that needs to be called out and not tolerated.

Compare that MBA gobbledygook with how CEO Jeff Lorberbaum spoke about the strategy for extraordinary growth at Mohawk Industries. Lorberbaum built his family's original $10,000 investment into the world's largest floor-covering company with almost $8 billion in annual sales. I spent hours interviewing Lorberbaum and was blown away by his unique combination of common sense and plain language, making complex business issues simple enough for someone in junior high school to comprehend.

Of Mohawk's highly effective and successful marketing plan, Lorberbaum says, "In our business [floor coverings] salespeople in floor covering stores want to control the conversation with the customer and also want their own life to be grief free, so they will never suggest products that cause complications or create customer disappointment. What we did was change our service model at the factory to be incredibly fast and reliable, so an installer gets what the customer needs within a day of the order being written. We don't let salespeople in carpet stores down, and that confidence in Mohawk is why retail salespeople prefer our company."

Anything confusing about "We exist to never let down the people who sell what we make"? I don't think so! Lorberbaum makes a strong business case; no gibberish or buzzwords are required. His approach to risk taking is similarly simple and clear.

"When an opportunity to acquire a good business comes along, you need to take advantage of the situation," he says, "but you never bet the farm. One year we bought five companies. It would have been impossible to get our culture of efficiency and simplicity integrated. So we let the existing management teams continue to run things and accepted their results until we were capable of making changes."

Leaders like Jeff Lorberbaum know keeping things simple and transparent keeps everyone engaged. "Most people are confused with the complexities. What I do is to *oversimplify* everything. That forces me to think things through and allows my people to concentrate on being more adaptive."

If you're not certain that you've managed simplicity in your communications, try asking a teenager to review your business plan summaries, guiding principles, and other communications to see if he or she can understand what you're saying. I asked a friend's daughter to take a look at a draft of a book chapter I had written. She read it and told me, "Sometimes I think you write stuff just to prove how smart you are." I had her highlight every phrase that struck her that way and I rewrote them all. Now I think of that criticism every day to help me make everything simple. Strong leaders don't need to use jargon to explain what they want—they explain everything in clear language so that every member of their organization understands their assignments and the ultimate purposes, principles, and goals of their company.

Make It Okay to Make Mistakes

When a missile launch went disastrously wrong at the World War II German rocket-development facility led by Wernher von Braun, an engineer quickly fessed up to his error—and received a bottle of champagne from his boss for his honesty. Von Braun knew if he humiliated or fired that technician, he would actually be promoting future cover-ups, costing his organization time and money. With his response, he made it okay to admit mistakes.

While interviewing Charles Koch, CEO of Koch Industries, I learned that in his company, the right to make decisions is based on the amount of knowledge someone has in a particular subject area and not by his or her place in the hierarchy. As an example, he told me the story of a young man who had been empowered to make a several-billion-dollar bet on behalf of the company. I was frankly stunned that someone so young had been entrusted with so large a responsibility.

"Why would you allow a twenty-seven-year-old to make such a huge decision?" I asked.

"That's simple," he said. "That young man had more knowledge about the area we were investing in than anyone else in the company, including me."

"But what if he'd made the wrong decision?" I asked.

"Well," he replied, "I guess we would have had a very bad year. It wouldn't have bankrupted us, but it wouldn't have been fun, but just think how much we would have learned if it had been the wrong decision."

Bob Engel of CoBank thinks the boss admitting his or her mistakes makes it okay for everyone to be more transparent. "The CEO needs to stand up and say, 'Hey, look, I got this one wrong. But we're going to get it right.' The amount of trust that builds is phenomenal."

Making mistakes isn't a sign of poor leadership—and allowing your team to make, report, and learn from mistakes in a united, fast-moving environment *is* a sign of great leadership. This was made clear in a surprising study published by Professor Amy Edmondson of Harvard in 2004 about empowered decision making in one of the most high-stakes environments we know: a hospital.

Preventable medical errors cost more than one hundred thousand lives and in excess of $20 billion annually; if adjusted to include the quality of life years lost by those who die, the total financial impact is estimated to be almost one trillion annually. Professor Edmondson studied critical care decisions in medical teams to find the roots of these errors. She expected to find that well-led teams were more reliable and produced fewer errors but in fact found just the opposite. Well-led teams with healthy relationships among all team members made *more* mistakes than less skilled leaders made with their teams. But upon looking more closely, what this revealed was that well-led teams with open, trusting, frequent communication among all the members reported their mistakes while defensive, distrusting, and dysfunctional teams led by punitive managers underreported errors, covered up mistakes, or blamed someone else. That's how they were able to score so low for medical errors.

"Good judgment comes from experience. Experience, unfortunately, often comes from exercising bad judgment," said the sage and humorist Will Rogers. Until you stop your organization from thinking, *Mistakes mean I'm stupid,* you're doomed to think slower and move even slower. Fast companies gain velocity by making it okay to make mistakes, by being careful to learn from their failures.

Bench "Captain Hindsight"

When the father of one of my associates died of esophageal cancer last April, my associate said, "If his doctors had checked for cancer when he first complained of acid reflux and hiccups, he might still be alive."

When NBC reported in 2004 that President Bush had been sent a memo more than a month before the September 11 attacks saying that Al Qaeda had reached America's shores and set up a support system for its operatives and that the FBI had detected suspicious activity that might involve a hijacking plot, politicians said, "Bush should have ordered more intelligence."

Things always seem so obvious in hindsight.

Hindsight is a scientific discovery of a cognitive bias that afflicts all of us. It comes from our strong desire to make sense of an often confusing and complex world (a good thing) and our inability to realize how easy it is to connect the dots *after* you know what happened (a very bad thing).

Daniel Kahneman, winner of the 2002 Nobel Prize in Economics and author of *Thinking, Fast and Slow*, studied our hindsight bias and the negative effect it has on thinking and acting fast. As he wrote, "Decision makers who know they are likely to have their actions scrutinized with hindsight are driven to be more bureaucratic and show an extreme reluctance to take risks."

How many times have you been in a meeting to go over your company's stumbles or flops from last year and a certain someone says, "I knew it all along" or "You could see the writing on the wall" or any other platitude of twenty-twenty hindsight?

We call this person "Captain Hindsight." He often frames discussions about "foreseeing" missteps after the fact to pat himself on the back and promote himself as an oracle. He also does it to make others feel dumb. According to Kahneman's research, these Captain Hindsights will make any organization slow. You need to bench them before their smug finger-pointing and constant Monday-morning quarterbacking slow you down irreparably.

End the Spin

According to a Towers Perrin (now Towers Watson) report, 55 percent of employees believe companies try too hard to put positive spin on issues, and 20 percent say their company is "not truthful." Even more damning, workers think their companies are much more likely to be honest with shareholders than with their workforces.

Fred Eppinger, Hanover's CEO (whom we met in chapter 1), equates being open with employees with being able "to admit your baby is ugly."

Though this might sound harsh, what Eppinger meant was that in business you've got to stop all the spin and politicking. (He's too nice a guy to ever say, "Your baby is ugly," to new parents.) His strategy as the new boss at Hanover Insurance was to be relentlessly truthful. So in his first months he met with everyone in the company, told it like it was, made promises, made sure other leaders at Hanover were also highly credible and extremely conscientious, and followed through relentlessly. I was in awe of his blunt manner and how quickly he got everyone engaged, taking urgent action.

Most people have great BS meters and are smart enough to know when they are hearing something authentic and when they are getting snowed. Every time you spin the truth or deceive them you make them a little more cynical. While being generally positive in your comments, putting things in the right perspective, and allowing those around you to save face is a far cry from spinning the truth, in our nanosecond culture you are better off being known as an honest, straight shooter than an evasive, double-talking politician.

Start Your Own "Great Game of Business"

Even if you're not in a position to share all the numbers with everyone in your business and teach them what those numbers mean, it's still time to be transparent and to teach everyone the facts of the great game of business. Prosperity, meritocracy, doing good to do well, putting the customer first, showing integrity, being transparent and honest . . . That's all just good business.

Begin every all-hands meeting in your department or company with a brief update of sales and how you're doing compared with the plan. Then, in brief, short segments, ask team members to quickly answer the following questions with a quick story or example:

- "Name a customer we helped yesterday and tell the story of how we did it." This reinforces the importance of the customer. There's a saying I use all the time, that if you call someone a horse ten times, they'll start looking for hay. If every day or every week you bring alive the importance of the customer, excellent customer-service will become part of your culture.

- "What efforts are going to be made today to get the team where you said you wanted to be?" This question and its answers will help reinforce the importance of urgency.

- "Did you have to deal with a crisis or problem since the last time we met? How was it handled?" The stories you hear in response to this question will become invaluable as, over time, you'll begin to discern patterns in your performance or strategy that can and should be addressed as a recurrence, not a one-off situation.

- "Share a great sales story from the previous day or week." This helps reinforce that everyone's job is to produce and subtly provides just the right amount of peer pressure, as everyone wants to have a great story to share.

- "Did any team member achieve a personal financial achievement?" Did someone buy a first home, save enough for a dream honeymoon, or retire student debt?

- A positive motivational thought for the day. There can't be enough of these. They can come from the boss, or people can be assigned to bring a great one for the next meeting. They provide powerful drivers for the team. Marketdata Enterprises estimates that more than $14 billion are spent on motivational books, DVDs, and seminars each year in the United States, for good reason; people want to feel good about themselves and what they do and they want to get better. As Zig Ziglar, the man who made motivation an industry, once said, "They say that motivation doesn't last and I agree. Showering doesn't last either which is why it's recommended every day."

Thank People for Their Vigilance

Several decades ago, the chairman and CEO of one of America's largest financial companies issued this extraordinary memo to be shared with the company's eleven thousand employees:

We need your help. . . . It is essential that once again we stress that we welcome every suspicion or feeling about something you see or hear that might not measure up to our standards of honesty or integrity. . . . If the doubt is justified the reporter will be rewarded handsomely. If the suspicion proves unfounded the person will be *thanked* for his or her vigilance and told to keep it up.

Forget the chain of command! That's not the way [our company] was built. If you think somebody is doing something off the wall or his/her decision-making stinks, go around that person and that includes me.

We want our people to tell us of boneheads or potential improprieties quickly!

This memo came from the late Alan "Ace" Greenberg, then head of Bear Stearns, and reprinted in his book *Memos from the Chairman*. In 2008 (seven years after Greenberg left the leadership circle) Bear Stearns, America's seventh-largest financial company, worth $6.7 billion on a Wednesday, accepted a fire-sale offer of just $236.2 million on Sunday. The head of the SEC blamed a "lack of confidence, not a lack of capital" for the incredible $6.4 billion loss in value in only four days. "Lack of confidence" sounds like a politician's way of saying people didn't believe a word they said and didn't trust them to do the right thing.

All I can wonder is, what's the likelihood that James Cayne, Greenberg's successor as CEO, believed as strongly as his predecessor in empowering employees to be watchful of Bear Stearns's ethics and unafraid of speaking truth to power?

When children ages nine and up are told to take one piece of candy from an unsupervised bowl of candy at Halloween, half will take more than one. But put that bowl in front of a mirror and 90 percent of kids stay honest. College students too are ten times less likely to cheat when they can see themselves in a mirror. The more closely we are watched, the better we behave!

In business the concept of the mirror is one of the powerful tools for getting things done right faster; 360-degree feedback (getting honest performance reviews from subordinates, associates in other departments, and other bosses, as well as your supervisor) is a great mirror, as is the offsider (the trusted associate who will tell you your baby is ugly). Best of all is a boss who has a direct line encouraging straight talk about everything.

"There's nothing you can do short of transparency to build a culture of urgency and growth," says Bob Engel, who has forged a new way of doing business in the financial services industry. "Forget the old way, where a few honchos had the information and tried to control things. That stuff is going to ruin your brand, give you a poor reputation, and when something bad happens you'll get a cover-up, which is always worse. You get trust, engagement, and a culture of urgency from transparency."

FAST TASKS

- Read Jack Stack's book *The Great Game of Business: The Only Sensible Way to Run a Company.*
- Make a promise to yourself to work relentlessly to end cynicism one person and one situation at a time. Tell everyone that your goal is transparency, and then give him or her permission (and maybe the occasional bottle of champagne) to tell you when you've strayed.

- Figure out how all your workers create value, determine how their contribution can be calculated, and meet with them individually to set measurable goals and track their progress. SSM did this by painstakingly defining what it really meant to provide "exceptional health care," then creating a yardstick that measured each of the five attributes that separated an exceptional provider from the average health care company. It focused on getting every department head in the organization to detail what his or her unit could do to help the effort to become exceptional, set measurable goals for every activity that contributed to SSM's achieving those five "exceptionals," and started tracking performance for each person and each day.

While there is no one-size-fits-all formula for calculating how each member of your workforce creates value, there's no job title where the amount of value created can't be determined with some out-of-the-box thinking and a little common sense.

Ultimately, the only reason for being in business is to find, keep, and grow the right customer, and that's accomplished only by growing, building, or manufacturing something, selling something produced by others, or providing a service. The only justification for hiring or having employees, therefore, is that they are the ones actually performing the building, manufacturing, growing, selling, and/or servicing or supporting those who perform those tasks. A job exists only to *do* or to support *doers*.

To visualize this, draw your organizational chart in pyramid form. Then draw a big smiley face—representing a single customer—outside the pyramid. You should be able to connect a line from that smiley face to any job title on the chart and answer the question, "How does this position create economic value?"

If you're unable to come up with a satisfactory answer for how a specific position within your company creates value, you probably have a bureaucratic mess on your hands and should start by eliminating the position.

- Select three tactics for gaining and achieving transparency from those listed in the chapter and implement them in the next week. Once that's done, start adding the others.

CHAPTER FIVE
Systematize Everything

RELIABLE, REPEATABLE, AND DURABLE

In early 2014 I spent a day in one of Ball Corporation's many manufacturing facilities. The plant I visited makes recyclable aluminum cans for beer and soda products—lots of them, seven million every day in just the one plant. That works out to about 54,000 cans per day per person for each of the plant's 130 workers.

It was fascinating to watch huge rolls of recycled aluminum being quickly moved into place, cut into small circles, given a quick but soft vertical punch to stretch them into cans, finished off with a beveled top, and then coated with the logo of the beer or soft drink they'd contain. Each step took a small fraction of a second. Before making their way out the back doors of the plant, the cans were briefly stacked on pallets that soared as high as the eye could see. Very organized, extremely efficient, and superfast; exactly the way things are meant to be done.

After I left the facility, I couldn't stop thinking about the efficiency and effectiveness of this effort. During my time there, I saw only two or three "bad" cans pop off the line, a minuscule percentage. How did so few people produce such a huge volume of error-free products in such a short amount of time? How were they able to coordinate every step and wring out every bit of waste, cutting unnecessary minutes and seconds from the arrival of raw materials, the process of making the can, and the mass customization necessary to meet customer needs and deliver to every Ball client?

The answer, of course, was something we all take for granted today: systematization. For more than one hundred years smart people have been getting together and systematizing every process in manufacturing, with each generation reexamining and refining the systems designed by its predecessors. The constant improvement in systematization is the result of the concepts of scientific management, inspired by total quality management, Six Sigma, and kaizen continuous improvement. When systematization is expertly executed, as the folks at Ball Corporation (among thousands of others) do it, it's fascinating to watch and sheer artistry in motion.

Over the last seven years, spurred by the financial meltdown of 2007 and global recession of 2008, high-speed companies have connected some dots that their slower and less adaptable competitors have not. The most successful companies understand that to make every part of business more reliable, productive, and teachable, to quickly and dramatically speed things up and improve results for customers, workers, and leadership, they need to systematize *everything*.

"Systematize everything" doesn't mean just automating and organizing every process that happens on the factory floor. It means setting up reliable, repeatable practices for everything in the sales and marketing departments, in research and development, in HR, and even in the strategy-setting and innovation activities of the CEO and other C-suite executives.

The steps of systematization are standard for any job at any level. High-speed companies start with a clear, specific, and measurable outcome and then examine the actions that currently produce the outcome, consulting data and history and looking for waste (of time or money) or gaps in the outcomes achieved. Then, by asking lots of questions, considering a lot of fresh ideas, and consulting its guiding principles, the company aims to map out the best way to get to a desired outcome.

No matter how smart you are, how advanced your education is, or how fast your brain computes in complex situations, systematization makes you faster, cheaper, and better. As Alfred North Whitehead, mathematician and process philosopher, observed, "Civilization advances by extending the number of important operations which we can perform without thinking about them."

It's just common sense. Yet while everyone loves the theory of systematizing people and processes, most absolutely hate the idea that someone might systematize *them* or *their* work. And the smarter people are, the loftier their positions, the more they hate the thought of their jobs being systematized. It's the great disconnect in business today—which points to a great opportunity for you to create a competitive advantage and end up with a high-speed company.

When Systematization Is a Matter of Life or Death

To understand just how much the smartest, most well-intentioned people resist being systematized, consider the following.

Almost two million infections occur annually in U.S. hospitals.

Among the most dreaded are central-blood-line infections, which are responsible for causing 35,000 hospital infection–related deaths each year. These infections are introduced through the intravenous catheters that deliver medication, nutrition, and fluids to patients in intensive care. Even for those who survive, a central-blood-line infection means weeks or months of debilitating treatments and painful side effects.

In 2001 Dr. Peter Pronovost, an MD with a PhD from Johns Hopkins, came up with a system that he believed could significantly decrease the number of central-blood-line infections in hospitals. He plotted five critical steps that help prevent these infections in critical care. Each step was simple and commonsense: Wash both hands before and after examining a patient, disinfect the patient's skin, use full barriers (gown, mask, and gloves), avoid placing the catheter in the groin, and remove unnecessary catheters.

Pronovost asked the nurses in his ICU to observe the doctors every time they inserted an IV catheter and check if each step was followed. After thirty days, the nurses totaled their checklists and discovered that doctors were skipping at least one of those steps for more than a third of all patients.

Next Pronovost asked the nurses to gently remind the doctors to follow all of the steps on the checklist or, if they thought it necessary, take charge and intervene when they saw a step being missed.

The results were dramatic: The infection rate quickly went down to *zero*. Pronovost and his colleagues computed that, during the trial period, adhering to this checklist had prevented forty-three infections and eight deaths and saved $2 million.

Pronovost created another checklist, this one for reducing postadmission pneumonia, and put it to work just like the first. The same unit reduced cases by 25 percent, saving an estimated twenty-one lives. Boosted by the results, Pronovost took his study on the road, expanding his systematization to Sinai-Grace Hospital in Detroit and testing out the checklist system in a facility with over seven hundred nurses, eight hundred doctors, five adult ICUs, and one infant ICU. In ninety days the infection rate there plummeted by 61 percent. Shortly after it adopted the checklist, Sinai-Grace's ICUs scored better than 90 percent of all ICUs nationwide for infection rates, saving fifteen hundred lives and $175 million.

At the beginning of Pronovost's experiments, many medical professionals were reluctant to embrace the checklists. "I didn't graduate at the top of my college class, spend four years in medical school, and do a five-year residency to fill out forms, told what to do, and be reminded to wash my hands" was a fairly typical reaction. It was a big fight to get physicians to accept his system.

Emotionally, most of us are like those doctors. When someone talks about making our personal job functions systematic, we don't hear concepts like *design* or *organize* and guiding values like *the best idea wins*. Instead we hear *shape up, tighten up, standardize,* and *regulate.* We imagine the worst of circumstances: being handed a narrow list of robotic tasks and responses that squeeze the spontaneity, creativity, and individuality out of our day while being relentlessly micromanaged by the know-less-than-us process police at headquarters. *We know what we need to do,* most people think. *Just leave us alone to do it.*

In fact, two of the world's most innovative companies have expressed opposing views on the idea of systematizing their innovation activities.

Eric Schmidt, former CEO of Google, adamantly believes innovation cannot be systematized. "Measuring it would choke it off altogether," he said. But Procter & Gamble's CEO, A. G. Lafley, believes it can be done. "It is possible to measure the yield of each process, the quality, and the end result," he says. He's proven his theory by creating systematic programs like "Living It," "Working It," and "Connect and Develop" to innovate better, leaner, and faster.

While we understand what Google's former CEO was worried about, our research has pushed us to Lafley's way of thinking. The *right kind* of systematization efforts don't strangle innovation or creativity. They actually free people and organizations up to be more creative, be more innovative, and adapt faster. Systems allow fast scaling and don't require reinventing the wheel every time something unexpected happens. I suspect Google will discover that systematization helps continual innovation as it, like P&G, approaches its 177th anniversary.

What's a System?

Good systems have four components:

- **They offer the best way to achieve a specific outcome.**

  It might be the way a shipment is packed, weighed, and measured to cut down on breakage, how phone calls are answered and directed to help create more demand, how a checklist is completed prior to a surgical procedure to reduce infections, or the way a customer's problems are escalated from tier 4 to tiers 3, 2, and 1 to keep more customers and reduce defections. The list of ways to achieve a given outcome is as big as your goals.

- **They require that everyone receive training.**

  Once you've determined how best to perform a task, you must teach it to everyone who will be involved in that system and explain the benefits derived from everyone's performing the task exactly the same way.

- **They don't allow deviation.**

For a system to work consistently, you must not tolerate deviation. If it's agreed that all outpatient surgical procedures will be preceded by a ten-point checklist, the nurse or doctor can't be excused for not following the program and doing it *his* way. You must constantly acknowledge and celebrate the wins achieved by your systematization, and when significant revenue gains or cost savings are realized, it's appropriate to share some of the spoils with the team members. Charts on walls plotting progress, congratulatory mentions in employee communications, small pins to be worn as badges of honor are all ways to get and keep people on board. The best disincentives for the staff members and managers who can't accept your system are a bit of counseling first and an old-fashioned firing next. (Your hiring "system" should have a way to test candidates for their fitness to a systematized business culture.)

- **They offer a baseline for continual improvement.**

Data, experience, and suggestions from the people performing the tasks are regularly weighed in an effort to make the systematization even better. Empirical data will allow you to tweak the systematization, and experiences of and suggestions from those performing the work should be regularly considered and implemented.

CREATING AND CASCADING SYSTEMATIZATION

In 2001 *Fortune* magazine named Anand Sharma a "hero of American manufacturing" for his expertise in systematizing. He had so quickly and dramatically upped the productivity of more than five hundred companies, including Dell, Pella, Maytag, Sealy, Caterpillar, CVS, and Gilead, that people had begun calling him "Maestro."

In a world where half of all great new ideas for improving business typically fail, Sharma succeeded nine out of ten times. How?

Sharma told me it's not because he's got a better mousetrap (he's a disciple of Lean Sigma), nor does he work with a more willing audience. Sharma succeeds when he systematizes, at more than twice the rate of other consultants, because *he has a system for the process of systematizing.*

His aha moment came when he realized that every time he failed to systematize successfully, there was one common element. "It was never that the systematization wasn't critically necessary or that our plan wasn't well thought out," he says. "It was always the human factor; it was always resistance to change." To combat this, Sharma identified four simple steps that guarantee he'll get the closest thing to flawless follow-through anybody has ever seen:

- Involve the top dogs.
- Select your fastest people.
- Choose a "wow" event.
- Follow through quickly.

Let's look at how this works.

Involve the Top Dogs

When you finish reading the following anecdote, you're going to think that I made it up and that it could not possibly have taken place. To the contrary, I assure you it's the truth, and each time I tell the story I painfully relive every sad moment.

I'd been hired by the CEO of a large Australian railroad to assist in crafting a new vision, mission, and KRAs (key result areas) for the company. The first daylong meeting with the company's top twenty-five key leaders was held off-site in a hotel. My associate Larry Haughton and I showed up early to greet and introduce ourselves to the participants as they arrived. We immediately sensed varying levels of nervousness and apprehension. These were railroad guys whose lives were possibly about to be turned upside down. The CEO considered the work so important that mobile phones and devices were collected and deposited in a basket. Promptly at eight thirty she called the meeting to order.

The CEO was smart and personable. She dutifully greeted everyone, explained the vital importance of the work we were about to embark on, and made a compelling case for the need to transform the company and the consequences of its not happening. She introduced Larry and me, nicely setting up our credentials.

Then she smiled wide and said, "Well, I'm going to leave you now and go and do what CEOs do. I wish you all the best in your important work. Remember, the future of the company is in your hands." With that, she gathered her coat, purse, and papers and sashayed out the door.

I was shocked and dumbfounded. How could someone bring the top leadership of a company together to do the most important work they'd ever undertake, spend huge money bringing the experts in, and then go MIA?

Having never been blindsided like that before, I slowly made my way to the front of the room, feeling anger, suppressed rage, massive amounts of adrenaline, and utter disappointment surging through my body. As I stood speechless in front of the room, wondering what to say and how to begin, everyone could sense my discomfort. Finally one guy (who had been the presumed new CEO until the surprise announcement that the board was hiring an outsider) raised his hand and said, "May I ask a question?" I nodded.

"What the &%$# just happened?" he asked. "Can someone tell us what that disappearing act was all about?" Of course, no answer would have been acceptable and no explanation believable. We'd just experienced firsthand the biggest abdication of executive responsibility we'd ever see in our lifetimes.

Though we tried to save the day, putting on our games faces and building a plan to help save and revitalize the company, our efforts were half measures at best. It seemed as though all the oxygen had been sucked out of the room. The plan we finally put together didn't get implemented in the end. How could it, when the top dog wasn't involved in its creation? In the sixty seconds it had taken the CEO to say good-bye and walk out of the room, she had deeply disappointed her top twenty-five leaders, showed her true colors, and mortally wounded herself. Her fate was effectively sealed. Another CEO soon replaced her.

There are three critical reasons why the top man or woman must be part of the systematization efforts:

1. They and they alone negotiate the expectations outside the firm.

    Naysayers are everywhere, and often the most damaging are outside investors, outside analysts, and pundits in the financial press. Only the CEO can negotiate the expectations of these outsiders and keep their negativity at bay. Anand Sharma saw firsthand how a detached CEO mishandled the wolves from Wall Street. The result was disaster.

    "This CEO was a showman," Sharma explains. "He was so excited about the systematization, he told all the Wall Street analysts what the organization was planning to do and his anticipated goals."

One quarter later, a young analyst came back and asked him about the results for the previous three months. He had done a quick bit of math and suggested that if the twelve-month goal was x, then the current quarter's progress should be x divided by four.

"Results from systematization can't be plotted on a straight line," Sharma says. "There are learning curves, setbacks, and unexpected obstacles. He'd have known that if he was part of the implementation, but instead he was on the sidelines. Because of his lack of firsthand experience, he let Wall Street paint him into a corner instead of taking charge and negotiating their expectations." And you know what happened next. When he fell short, Wall Street said, "I think the sky may be falling," and the CEO never got the rope he needed to make the plan work.

2. They have to power to protect the tender green shoots of success.

"I've got fifty million reasons to say I loved your book," an executive wrote to me. He'd used a chapter from *It's Not the Big That Eat the Small* to catalyze a new system that uncovered $50 million of uncollected receivables at his technology company. His CEO was so impressed that he announced to the whole company, "If 10 percent of our people had this guy's initiative, all our problems would be solved!"

When this exuberant executive wrote to me eighteen months later to say he had been let go in the latest restructuring, I was shocked. He wasn't. "When the senior VPs two levels above me got wind of my system, they made me a marked man. You've heard the saying 'The reformer has enemies in all those who profit by the old order, and only lukewarm defenders in any who would profit by the new order,' haven't you?"

There is only one person with the power to protect the tender green shoots of a systematization's success from the enemies of reform—and that's the man or woman at the top. One of the responsibilities of the person at the top is to be involved and stay involved in the initiatives they undertake and to protect young and emerging talent from becoming victims of those who would prefer to keep things the way they are. Otherwise, they're simply paying lip service to supporting their organization.

3. The CEO must also be the CGO—Chief Grit Officer.

Grit is the ability to maintain momentum long after the mood has passed. You can feed your grit by feeling the excitement of your "wow" event firsthand.

If the head of the division (and this applies only to executives who are able to act unencumbered by the home office), owner, or CEO fails to take ownership and isn't actively engaged in any major transformation or systematization effort, the organization will be lucky to achieve lukewarm results and, more likely than not, will be doomed to fail.

Anand Sharma warns against this as well. "Unless the top dog leads the effort," he says, "it's likely to get derailed during the first crisis or the first time an adverse condition is encountered. It's vitally important to continue when something goes wrong—not abandon it."

Getting a front-row seat as great companies are systematizing and witnessing the aha moments of great leaders as they succeed are two of the perks of my professional life. Here are the ways I've seen leaders get those aha moments in systematizing. Let's explore how they've done it—and how you can use these techniques in your own organization.

Select Your Fastest People

As pointed out before, 83 percent of people will sit on their hands at the introduction of any change in routine. The reason more people won't support new initiatives is because they are waiting to see that it's safe before they get off the sidelines and join in.

Now, a glass-half-empty type of leader might say, "What am I supposed to do when four out of five people won't pitch in?" The glass-half-full person sees that number and says, "Seventeen out of every hundred employees will follow my lead immediately? Terrific!"

Once you've decided to launch your systematization overhaul, you need to find enough seventeen percenters to pitch in and make it work. You'll learn how to identify your seventeen percenters in upcoming chapters, but you probably already know who these people are; they're the people who welcome change, show initiative, and are the first ones to raise their hands and shout, "Pick me, boss, pick me!"

Choose a "Wow" Event

To melt resistance and get people off their hands, you need a powerful success story, one that will make people believe in the power of systematization and get them amped to apply systematization in other parts of the business. It can be small, just not insignificant. The idea is to get people to say, "Wow."

One of Sharma's "wow" events cut the time necessary to produce one critical component on an assembly floor at Maytag by 84 percent. At Lantech, a manufacturer of large shrink-wrap machines, one of these wow events quadrupled inventory turn, sales per employee increased by 80 percent, and many millions of dollars suddenly appeared on the bottom line. And when Sharma's team reduced the number of employees necessary to support one leg of an assembly line at Caterpillar from twelve workers to just two and helped the plant's management reassign all ten now-redundant workers to new roles, the brass, the coworkers, and the unions all said, "Wow!"

Picking a wow event is a critical and difficult task. "You must be very smart about selecting your wow event," Sharma cautions. "Most managers are overconfident; they'll take on impossible timetables or promise miracles across the entire enterprise." Sharma learned how to organize wow events around unnecessary motion, inventory overloads, high defection rates, and other kinds of waste that others had missed in one typical location. He'd draw up process diagrams, review past successes, and ask great questions that unearthed big opportunities for radical transformation.

You can't just dream big here and not have the results to instill the importance of systematization in your team. Don't think that anyone will simply respect your bravery as you take on the impossible—it's not enough. And don't believe your teams have the grit necessary to overcome early setbacks. They don't. Every company has many people in the shadows just waiting to whisper, "I told you this idea couldn't work." All optimism is fragile; success feels like a fluke and every setback appears to be a sign that the sky is falling. When you select a wow event, *know* you can make it work.

Follow Through Quickly

The late Yoshiki Iwata taught Sharma how to systematize a leaner and more improved way of doing anything in only five days. He called it "kaizen blitzkrieg," which combined taking apart and putting a process back together in a better way (*kaizen*) with a quick and overpowering attack (*blitzkrieg*). Iwata's innovation helped get the Toyota Production System up and running in partner companies four times faster than it had been implemented at Toyota itself.

Sharma realized that Iwata's kaizen blitz had a hidden benefit for overcoming human resistance to change. There are always a few, in every organization, who see it as their job to be the antibodies in the company's immune system. They assume the role of skeptic and pessimist and stand against new ideas or changes to the organization, just as the antibodies in your body oppose any helpful transplant.

One of my friends calls these people "the Mayors of Coolertown." Coolertown is the space in the break room around the watercooler. That's where these politicians hold their whispering town halls, explaining to anyone who will listen why things can't change and won't work out as leadership wants. "We tried that before and it didn't work," they say. "Besides, things are different here than there [where the system has worked]." They spread uncertainty and share feelings of being at risk. They want to keep everyone sitting on their hands. "Let's commission a study," they say, "just to be safe."

Sharma knows that, by nature, these people move slowly and hate speed. So when you actually follow through fast, you can catch them flat-footed. Before they are able to create fear, uncertainty, and doom, you've already provided real examples of success and exuberant advocates from your organization's rank and file.

The Coolertown mayors can't say, "It didn't work" or "We're different." The facts are there to be seen. And just like a doctor, you've protected your new idea from being rejected by the immune system.

Let People Ask "Dumb" Questions

"I love using cross-functional teams in my wow events because outsiders and inexperienced people ask those good, *dumb* questions," Pat Lancaster, former CEO of Lantech, told me. "Good *dumb* questions are the questions that force you to explain your assumptions and embedded routines. They're great for clearing out the cobwebs and getting us to address the heart of the matter."

Questioning long-held assumptions can appear to waste time. That's especially common in the 80 percent of companies that don't keep track of their rates of follow-through. Memories are convenient and they mostly confirm how awesome a given company thinks it is. Cold research says otherwise.

Probably the best dumb question anyone can ask is "Why?" It's so powerful that Taiichi Ohno of Toyota made asking "why" part of the company's systematization of continual improvement. The "Five Whys" (defining, measuring, analyzing, improving, and controlling) are designed to get decision makers to look for the root cause of a problem before any solution is implemented. Over the years, and with a few nuanced enhancements, using "why" to find root causes has proven to be the fastest, most efficient way to prevent recurrence of a bad outcome.

Always Let the Best Idea Win

When John Maynard Keynes said, "It is better for your reputation to fail conventionally than to succeed unconventionally," he had to be talking about life in an old-fashioned bureaucracy. Any approach that doesn't include letting the best idea win makes no sense in a modern business. With relentless competition, customers prepared to stop doing business with you at any moment, and every misstep a potential disaster, the best idea, even if it is unconventional, must win.

Sadly, more often than not, it's still the boss's idea, the old idea, the competition's idea, or the celebrity CEO's idea that wins at a lot of companies. Don't let that be who you become.

Search for good ideas relentlessly. Ask, "Who has solved this problem or a problem with similar features?" and bring in outside voices. Adopt an inquiry mode of discovery, asking yourself and your team questions that draw out possibilities rather than shut down people who express unconventional opinions. Ban negativity in your problem-solving discussions. Statements like "I'm fundamentally opposed to that" or "We tried that and it didn't work" or "Let me play devil's advocate" have no place in this world.

Perfect Is the Enemy of the Good

"It is much less acceptable now at our company to do nothing," Mel Haught, former CEO of Pella, told me, "than to do something and go back later and make changes." He was very proud that he had changed his company's paralyzing culture of perfectionism.

School teaches us that there are right answers and that smart people have those answers memorized. Remember how embarrassed you were when you raised your hand and had the wrong answer? Classmates laughed, the teacher frowned, and you said to yourself, *Keep quiet unless you have the perfect answer.*

Those who act as the antibodies in the company culture use those painful memories from school to kill the changes necessary in systematization. They will ask, "What if . . . ?" and suggest more research. They operate under the myth that if you take your time and gather enough data, you can find the perfect strategy.

The best systems in business are made by doing. Napoleon said, "One jumps into the fray and then figures out what's next."

Involving your people in determining the best way to do something, teaching everyone how to perform the task(s) in the prescribed way, making certain there is no deviation, and using the system as a baseline for future improvement will provide you huge competitive advantages over the competition and allow the organization to spend more of its time thinking fast and moving faster.

FAST TASKS

- Put together a short list of seven to ten of your seventeen percenters, those who welcome and support new initiatives and change within your company. Hopefully your group will include a tribal elder, relatively new hires with fresh sets of eyes, technical and non-technical staff and managers, and maybe even a customer who is one of your company's apostles. Ask them to carefully read this chapter.

- Gather this group for a half-day off-site session to build a list of things in the business that can be improved through systematization. The exercise will be fun and the potential list will surprise you. Schedule a ninety-minute get-together a week later to come up with a prioritized list of targets for systematization that could have a significant impact on your business.

- During the meeting, ask your seventeen percenters, one by one, to present their cases for the first areas they recommend for systematization and select one that will have a clear goal, be measurable, and have a "wow" effect on the workforce. Always select the wow events that have both impact and a likelihood of success—don't start with reluctant people or the worst division in the company.

- Select six to ten people from the area or process that's going to be systematized, bring them together, announce the goal and the plan to systematize, explain why and what's in it for them, and invite them to be the "systematizers." Add a few people from the original group whose thinking and performance in the first meetings distinguished them. Ask the group to begin gathering data, stories, and anecdotal evidence about the area or process to be systematized. Schedule a several-hour session whose purpose is to map out and select the system.

- At some point during your next session, when your map is in place and someone asks when you're planning on implementing it, channel the spirit of Anand Sharma, breathe deeply, and say, "Right now! Let's do it!" Then do it!

- As soon as you've completed and celebrated, it's time to do it again. Gather your seventeen percenters and pick another area to systematize. And then another, and another.

CHAPTER SIX
Communication

EXPLORATION AND DISCOVERY

If you believe that one reason high-speed companies are fast is because they do a good job of communicating from the top down, you're not wrong. But if you believe terrific top-down communication is the result of the "I talk and you listen" practiced by executives at most companies, you're mistaken.

The ways that most companies communicate with their workforces have been an abject failure. If you doubt that, consider the following.

- 72 percent of all U.S. workers are either disengaged (saying they are unlikely to invest any discretionary effort in organizational goals or outcomes) or actively sabotaging their workplaces (spraying their negativity over their coworkers), according to Gallup research in 2013. In Australia it's 76 percent; in Latin America, 79 percent; in Western Europe, 86 percent; and in Asia, 87 percent.

- 53 percent of all employees have little confidence in their senior leaders and think their senior leaders have little interest in them, according to the 2012 Global Workforce Study by Towers Watson. That finding echoes an earlier workforce study where two out of three employees described their executives as poor communicators.

- When University of Chicago's General Social Survey asked millennials, "Can most people be trusted?" 84 percent said no. And it's not just the young generation that doesn't trust leaders, supervisors, or coworkers. Across all age groups trust in others is at its lowest level since General Social Survey's first report in 1972.

Why Top-Down Communication Fails

Our collective failure at effective communication isn't from a lack of trying. We've all been schooled in communication tactics like employing the compliment sandwich, mirroring, using clever acronyms, repeating the other person's name, making constant eye contact, and speaking assertively.

One-size-fits-all tactics like these have made our trust and belief problems worse. Audiences roll their eyes when a presenter uses those communication techniques. Most top-down communication misses the mark because, as well intended as the constant flow of newsletters, memos, virtual town-hall meetings, and tweets is, they don't speak to the wants, needs, ambitions, hopes, and fears of the people on the receiving end. These are, in the true sense of the word, irrelevant and frequently seen as a nuisance. Top-down communication has to be tailored to the recipient, so that she sees real value in it for her and believes any information shared will help her finish her tasks and projects faster or get to where she wants to go.

Good leaders understand it's important to know the story of everyone who reports to them so they can match skills, talents, and aspirations to assignments and roles. That's the way it's been done for decades among the cadre in the C suite, where leaders know one another and look out for one another, helping and boosting one another along and celebrating their mutual successes.

Great leaders understand it's vitally important that every leader and manager in the company take the same keen level of interest in *all* the people who report to him or her, not just those who share office space on the top floor.

But the *greatest* leaders, those committed to building faster organizations, know there's no way to lead anybody anywhere—much less to do so quickly—without knowing where each person wants to go, how soon he wants to get there, what he is willing to invest to get to the destination, and his level of commitment to the team.

The world's most accomplished and enduring leaders—those whose leadership withstands the test of time, like Lincoln, Churchill, Gandhi, Meir, and Mandela—derived unrivaled satisfaction from helping others get to where they wanted to go. In the process, groups of people who saw a real possibility of achieving their greatest desires worked to help the leader achieve his or her objectives. None of this can happen without taking the time to learn people's stories. Great communication from the bottom to the top is merely democratizing something that's been a little secret among the top ranks for years.

A Master Class in Connection

I met one of the greatest business communicators I've ever known at the very beginning of my career, though I was young and failed to recognize his incredible skills at the time. He truly demonstrated the secret to inspiring, motivating, believable communications. If you want to create a culture of urgency, grow employee engagement, and get more belief and trust in your leadership, you need to read his story and make it your own.

When I first met this man, I was just twenty years old. Every morning I woke at 3:00 a.m. to prepare for and host a morning radio show while carrying a full load of credits in school with a double major in political science and communications. I was always dashing back and forth between the university campus and the radio station, where I was also the general manager and responsible for making sales calls on advertisers every day as well. Things were always extremely busy. There weren't many hours for sleep, no one told me that the word "party" had become a verb, and finding time to study and write papers was always a problem—but I was young and life was good.

When I walked into the radio station's offices one day, the receptionist spotted me and said, "Oh good, you're here. There's someone on the phone calling for you from Detroit." I guessed the call was from an advertising agency, so I picked up the phone and said, "Hello, this is Jason. How can I help you?"

The voice on the other end said, "This is Myron P. Patten calling from the Patten Company in Detroit. Do those names ring a bell?"

Thinking I was about to get some big-city attitude from an ad buyer, I almost replied, "Sure, I've heard of Detroit." But instead I took a breath and said very nicely, "No, I'm sorry, those names don't ring any bells."

"A few weeks ago Dan, the manager of one of my radio stations, met you," he said, "and was so impressed that he drove four hundred miles to visit your radio station and spend a day with you. He suggested that I call about you possibly joining our company."

"Wow, that's very nice of you," I stammered, suddenly very self-conscious with all the people around me and not quite knowing what to say. "I'm honored, but I have a great job, love what I do, my owners are good to me and I wouldn't want to hurt their feelings, and I'm also going to school."

"I understand all those things," he said, "but it wouldn't hurt to get to know each other. So why don't I have an airplane ticket waiting for you for a flight this Friday afternoon from Marquette to Detroit? We can have dinner at my home, I can show you the company on Saturday morning, and you can fly home that afternoon. No one will even know you've been out of town."

So the next Friday afternoon, not having told anyone about the trip, I found myself feeling a little like I imagine a cheating spouse feels, surreptitiously picking up a ticket at the airline ticket counter, flying to Detroit, being met by Mr. Patten in a Cadillac as big as a boat, and going to his home to meet his wife and family. After a great meal, Mr. Patten and I sat down in the kitchen for a drink and out of the blue he asked me a question.

"Where do you want to end up?" he asked.

"What do you mean by 'end up'?" I replied.

"Where do you see your life taking you? What do you want to accomplish with your life's work?"

I was twenty years old and had never once considered the question he was asking. I was still years away from hearing (and rejecting) the Socrates quote that "an unexamined life isn't worth living." I was stumped.

"Just start by telling me some of your hopes and dreams," he prodded. "You have some of those, I bet."

I'm not sure what we were drinking, but I learned later that his family had changed their name to Patten from Padopoulos, so I'm guessing it was either Greek retsina or ouzo. I was feeling warmer and more comfortable by the moment and so—what the heck—I spewed.

I told him I'd grown up lower middle class but all my smart friends had come from families with money, and their parents had always treated me as though I weren't good enough to hang with their kids. I wanted to achieve financial success, have a family, a beautiful home, and financial security. My ultimate payback to those who'd treated me like a hayseed would be to never treat anyone badly because of their economic circumstances. I explained that young people had more to offer than they were given credit for, that I wanted to change things, and that I wasn't prepared to wait ten or fifteen years to be recognized and promoted. I told him what I was good at, what I wasn't good at (I was twenty so, in my mind, that list wasn't too long), and that I wanted to become a great business leader who treated people well. On and on it went (remember, he'd asked the question and fueled the discussion with Greek firewater). By the time my monologue ended, I'd told him all of my hopes and dreams.

Later that night at the hotel, I remember thinking that I'd said too much, had been too free with information, and was beginning to suspect there wasn't going to be a job offer forthcoming. That premonition turned out to be correct.

The next morning Mr. Patten and I visited the impressive

headquarters that housed the broadcasting, advertising, and international trade divisions of his company. I had several conventional job interviews with a few members of his leadership team. As he was driving me back to the airport, he said, "I'm sorry, Jason, my people really like you and so do I, but based on everything you told me last night and what you want to achieve, I don't have a job for you."

My heart plummeted. I've always been fiercely competitive, and being shot out of the water stung hard.

He paused a long time before adding, "But you have too many talents to pass up. Give me a few days to think about what you want to do with your life and I'll try to match that up with where the company is going, and I'll call you."

True to his word, three days later Mr. Patten called and explained what he'd decided. "Based on our long talk, my leaders getting to know you a little, and having had you checked out," he said, "we really don't have anything for you to run that will allow you to also go to school at night. But if you'll agree to join the company as my executive assistant and spend some time learning who we are and how we operate, we'll work together to build a plan for you that will allow you to go to school. We're certain that at some point there will be a match between your talents, what you want to achieve, and what we're building, and we'll have something for you to run and become a member of the senior leadership team."

I took the job. The next eighteen months were a whirlwind. I observed executive committee and board meetings, authored the company's first policy and procedures manual, filled in for department heads when they were absent, learned how to read financial statements, was sent on trips to help save clients who were threatening to leave, accidentally closed a few big deals along the way, headed the media and creative departments on an interim basis, was placed in charge of a congressional campaign (which we won, against all odds), attended classes at night, slept less than ever before, and, sadly, still never learned that "party" was a verb.

Mr. Patten had a special talent for tying the work I was doing back to all the things I'd told him in his kitchen the night we first met. The time I made my first sales trip (because none of the senior people thought there was a chance to close the business and it required being away for a holiday weekend), I brought back two big, signed deals, earning a sizable bonus check. Mr. Patten asked me what I was going to do with the money. I replied that I'd been eyeing a small foreign sports car. His response was "Well, that doesn't sound like the young man sitting in my kitchen who said he wanted financial security." I didn't buy the car and saved the money.

Another time we were walking to a nearby Chinese restaurant for lunch when an obviously down-on-his-luck street person hit us up for money. I made some kind of derisive remark. All Mr. Patten said was "Don't I recall you telling me that you would never judge people less economically fortunate than you?" and handed the guy a wad of bills.

Similarly, when an idea I'd had for a new advertising campaign had been shot down and he saw me sitting alone in my office, obviously bummed out, he walked in, sat down, and said, "You told me how much young people have to offer and you told me you were willing to fight for change. So why give up? Why not fight?" I did and, with a few tweaks to the campaign, eventually won.

It happened over and over again. Mr. Patten always brought me back to the things I'd told him I wanted to do. Each time he reminded me of my big dreams, his reminder made what I'd told him even more real, alive, and attainable.

Because he had taken the time and interest to learn not only my skills but also my hopes, fears, wants, needs, and aspirations, he knew how to lead me and help me move myself closer to where I'd told him I wanted to be. In opening up and revealing the real me to this person, I'd given him permission to lead me. In return, I worked harder, traveled farther, and did whatever needed to be done because I didn't want to disappoint my leader.

Patten wasn't an assertive speaker, yet I was overwhelmed with a feeling of confidence in him and his vision. Nor did he charm me with his charisma, yet to this day I've never felt more inspired by a leader. What Patten taught me is a strategy that works for everyone. It doesn't rely on your being a central-casting image of a commanding boss: You won't need a snappy PowerPoint or other presentation aids to get your team on board in this way.

Patten was just a normal, regular kind of guy. All he did was start me talking, listen, and discover everything he needed to know to be an effective leader to me.

Three Lessons from Myron Patten

Here are three things a leader can do to immediately become a more effective communicator, one better positioned to make the company faster.

1. Be interested, not interesting.

   In a famous scene from the film *Beaches*, Bette Midler's character sums up what's gone wrong in most of our business communications. "Enough about me. Let's talk about you," she says. "What do *you* think of me?"

   Myron Patten was a hugely accomplished entrepreneur, political strategist, and philanthropist. Years later I heard of his exploits recognizing and getting the right kind of politicians elected, of how his vision revolutionized retail marketing in the automobile business, and of how he made billions of dollars for his clients. He could have talked about himself and told stories worthy of a Hollywood movie script. But he didn't. In the first five hours we spent together, he never said anything about his accomplishments. He was too interested in hearing about me.

With him, I was the star. He was inquisitive and genuine; I never doubted that he cared about what I thought. He asked great questions that seemed to come off the top of his head. He steered me gently and got me to reveal everything.

People often ask me for the ten or twenty questions they need to ask to learn all about someone and his or her hopes for the future. "You don't need a list," I tell them. "You just need to be interested and curious."

William F. Buckley had a great take on how he got so good at being interested in others. "Ninety-nine percent of all people are interesting. The hundredth isn't," he said. "But even he's interesting because he isn't. In that sense you can never lose." I think Patten saw it that way too.

2. Don't just listen; hear.

Even when we listen, we do not necessarily hear. The reasons are part of human nature. Our brains process information four times faster than people speak, so as listeners we are easily distracted. We miss important clues and insights because we are so focused on our own agendas and defensive about our opinions. Most important, though we get a lot of instruction as undergraduates and graduates in writing and speaking, nobody shows us how to genuinely listen and really hear.

It's a lot of work to overcome our nature and become good listeners. We need the right prescription so we're able to listen and hear everything we are told.

It takes a lot of energy to really pay attention to someone. Take it from me: I've done over eleven thousand interviews with executives and entrepreneurs in the last fifteen years. A key to listening well is not trying to do too much. I thought I could do eight hours of interviews, five days a week. All I got was gobbledygook and sensory overload; I wasn't retaining or comprehending. As difficult as it may be, we need to slow down when we listen. Try to listen with your full attention for one conversation a day. You can expand from there.

Besides energy, you need the discipline to listen with an open mind. Procter & Gamble's CEO, A. G. Lafley, put it best: "People's default mode of communication is to advocate, to favor their own conclusions and point of view. To create the kind of dialogue we wanted at P&G we had to shift to something very different . . . from advocating to systematically inquiring about the thoughts and reasoning of peers."

At P&G they have developed a process for opening their minds and inquiring instead of advocating. According to Lafley, the process goes something like this: "First we instilled a different mind-set [among executives] that says, 'I have a view . . . but I may be missing something.' Second, as we listen, we paraphrase what we are told, saying, 'It sounds to me like you think this. Does that capture what you said accurately?' And last, we keep asking, 'I'm not sure I understand. . . . Could you tell me more?' to make sure there's no misunderstanding."

Finally, there's a good test I recommend to review your listening skills, adapted from one of the fathers of the short story, Guy de Maupassant. In giving direction to writers, he implored them, "Go into the streets and pick out a cab driver. Study him until you can describe him so that he is seen in your description to be an individual, different from every other cab driver in the world." I recommend you do the same for your business communication. Try to tell what you've heard and observed as an interesting, compelling story. If you can tell what you've learned from someone and describe him or her as an individual worthy of attention, you've listened well.

3. Use your head *and* your heart.

When we think about being businesslike, we typically think efficient, methodical, practical, and unenthusiastic. All those words suggest businesspeople need a wall between their head and their heart if they want to succeed. But that's all wrong. Great communicators tear down that wall in connecting with others.

Psychoanalyst Heinz Kohut, one of the originators of empathetic listening for professionals, defined empathy as "the capacity to think and feel oneself into the inner life of another." To think and feel we need to use both our heads and our hearts.

Patten used his head; there was no one in the company who knew the numbers better than he did. But he used a lot of heart daily, guiding everyone a step closer to where they'd told him they wanted to be. He was empathetic—and effective.

In 2001 Jörgen Sandberg wrote about the automobile engineers at the Volvo factory he recently had studied. The most effective group, he found, were those who imagined themselves as ordinary customers as they tested engines and made decisions about the final product. Empathy influenced the quality of their work.

Imagine how fast and powerful your team and company would become if each leader knew not only the talents but also the hopes, wants, needs, and dreams of each direct report. They would be able not just to match tasks with talents but to do so in a way that progressively moved people toward their personal goals and objectives. Engagement and speed scores would skyrocket.

CREATING AND CASCADING BETTER COMMUNICATION

My boyhood best pal Kenny Foster and I used to spend countless hours in an empty upstairs room in his house on Newberry Avenue, building almost-large-as-life cardboard mock-ups of the boat we were going to use to explore the world and discover new things. I bet you and your friends did something similar (there's a bit of the explorer in all of us). The most satisfying explorations you'll ever conduct are what I refer to as "discovery meetings." Here you'll get to hear and learn people's stories and in the process learn how to lead them to the achievement of their goals and ambitions. (Please note that I'd never actually use the phrase "discovery meeting" with someone I was about to meet, and I wouldn't advise you to use the phrase either. Rather, it's the frame of mind you're putting yourself into before the interaction, setting yourself to meet with someone you really don't know and learn about them, their talents, their aspirations, what they're trying to achieve in life and how you might be able to help get them there.)

While I've made every effort to fill this book with practical instructions for building a high-speed company, I am not going to provide a list of questions to ask during discovery meetings with your team. Can you imagine what would happen if tens of thousands of people started asking other people the same questions? Both the process and the questions would be seen as a manipulative exercise, the furthest thing possible from the truth. In addition to taking what you've already read to heart, consider the following suggestions for how to communicate in your company.

Check Yourself

The discovery conversation isn't a rote flight checklist you're making your way through. If someone isn't genuinely interested in learning about another person—and doesn't want to have the conversation for the right reasons—his or her lack of sincerity and authenticity will be immediately telegraphed.

This is a tough one for leaders; you may not like the person or may be so stressed that you don't have the interest or energy to really connect. But beware: People have really good BS meters. Don't try to fake sincerity. If you can't bring your head and your heart to the discovery conversation, you're better off postponing or getting someone to help.

Timing Is Everything

Don't try to have a discovery conversation in an office or cube without privacy. Open doors, constant interruptions, devices ringing and pinging, and people poking in for a quick response to a question aren't conducive to the flow you're trying to achieve. Comfortable, neutral seating is vitally important. If the boss is sitting behind his desk and the worker is in a guest chair in front of the desk, communication will be staged and stifled. I suggest getting out of the workplace altogether whenever possible.

Be Vulnerable

Because complete honesty and authenticity are so rare, a display of both is generally disarming. Most people will at least temporarily suspend any sense of disbelief when you approach them with the following: "Carol, I think I'd be able to be a better leader and help you get to where you want to go if I knew a little more about you and learned where you want to go and want you want to achieve in life. Can we spend some time talking about you?" In this case the two parties have both just made themselves a little vulnerable, the boss by saying she'd like to be a better leader and the employee by agreeing to the conversation. You're familiar with the line "When you get someone talking about themselves, the hardest part is to get them to stop," and it's true. People love to talk about themselves. This will be their opportunity to truly be heard, possibly for the first time in a long while.

Remember, It's Not About You

As you're asking questions, curb the urge to talk about you. At a minimum the conversation should be 90 percent the other person and 10 percent or less you. Remind yourself, *I can talk about me another time. Today's my chance to learn about someone else.*

Silences Are Golden

Be prepared to encounter and deal with natural pauses in the discovery conversation. The moment there's a pause, most people have a tendency to jump in and keep things moving. Early in my career a radio and television news producer told me, "Once you've asked a question and the person you're interviewing has answered the question, don't say another word. Let there be a pause and almost always the next words spoken by the person you're interviewing will be the best material." During pauses people are gathering their thoughts, trying to get the words right, analyzing how much they trust you, and wondering if you're someone worthy of sharing their dreams. Keep a muzzle on your mouth.

"And Then . . ."

Some of my best daylong interviews with CEOs and company owners have required asking only three questions: "Tell me the story of the company through your eyes," "Tell me your story," and "What's keeping you awake at night these days about your business?" The only other words I've had to use to keep the conversation going were "And then . . . ," "What happened next?" "Aha, that's fascinating," and "What's likely to happen if you do or don't do that?" This prompts them to keep speaking without guiding their revealing thoughts in any particular direction or making a bias known.

Repeat What You've Heard

When you hear something that's potentially important, use a small gesture to pause the conversation and say, "I want to make certain I understood what you just said. Did I hear correctly that ____?" When you repeat information, you'll stand a better job of remembering it. When the person you're listening to confirms that you heard correctly, what they've said almost becomes a silent pact between both parties, that you have heard them, understood them, and they will stand by their words no matter what.

Additionally, the competent paraphrasing of another is the single best device for scrubbing bias and advocacy out of your comprehension. It also offers proof to others that you can be trusted. "A competent paraphrase," says Jay Rosen, a highly regarded professor of journalism at NYU, "is where I tell you what you said, you hear it, and you recognize it saying: 'Yeah, more or less . . . I wouldn't use those words, but yes.' This is sometimes called fairness."

No Notes, Please

I still remember everything I've ever heard during all of my discovery meetings—and there have been many thousands of them. If you are genuinely interested, listen intently, and hang on to the edge of your seat waiting for the next part of the story, you don't need any notes and you'll remember everything you hear for the rest of your life. This isn't an interview . . . but that's what it will turn out to be if the other person sees you taking notes.

Be a Dream Catcher

Leaders shouldn't be afraid to use the word "dream" in their conversations. Everyone, no matter how superficially cynical he or she may be, has dreams. The only question is whether the person you're listening to trusts you enough to share them. Questions like "What would your dream job look like?" "Where do you dream about ending up in your career?" and "What would a dream assignment be?" are great ways to get people to reveal themselves.

Tie Their Goals to Yours

When people share their dreams and what they want to accomplish in their careers with their leader or manager, they provide her with everything she needs to know to be able to communicate downward with them more effectively. A statement like "Michael, I have a tough assignment for you that really needs to be completed in a hurry, and I truly believe it will take you a step closer to the next management opening we have" won't be seen as a carrot on the end of a stick but as evidence that the leader remembers what she was told.

Pete Carroll, coach of the Super Bowl–winning Seattle Seahawks and arguably the greatest collegiate football coach ever, once told me, "Leaders take people or groups of people where they really dream about going but couldn't or wouldn't get on their own." Carroll made it even clearer when he added, "Every player who ever walked on the field at USC wanted to win a national championship and every Seahawk wanted to win a Super Bowl. But they couldn't do it alone. It was my job to lead them there."

When you know what people want to achieve, you're able to (and should) employ every tactic of a great sports coach, just as Mr. Patten did to me and Pete Carroll does to his players: cajole, push, challenge, remind them of the championship they said they wanted to win, and passionately care about their getting to where they said they wanted to go.

What Are They Prepared to Invest?

Once you've truly listened and heard about their hopes, dreams, and aspirations, there's a final question you need to ask: "What are you willing to do, what are the things you're prepared to do to achieve what you say you want to achieve?" There are only a few things people can invest in themselves: time, energy, commitment, and money. You need to prod a little to learn how much time and energy they're prepared to commit in order to achieve their hopes and dreams. What skill sets do they think are necessary to get to where they want to go, and are they prepared to invest the time and energy to gain these? Are they prepared to invest money in a program of self-improvement to move them closer to their end goals? Their answers to questions about what they're prepared to commit and undertake will speak volumes about their character.

End Unproductive Perfectionism

On a rare occasion you'll find yourself listening to the dreams and hopes of someone whose skill sets don't give him a chance of getting to where he wants to go or achieving what he says he wants to achieve. When it happens, the leader needs to spend some time thinking about everything she's heard and then respond with the candor and honesty expected of true leaders.

First check to see if you are listening with both your head and your heart. Are you reading between the lines? Do you know what this person's outsized goals are really saying? Is he looking for love and expecting stature to fill that hole in his life? Is she trying to please an impossible parent instead of becoming her own definition of success? Is he just immature, or is he irreparably delusional and incapable of self-knowledge? Your conclusions will guide your response.

If you find that the person is deeply deluded, remember that you're not a miracle worker who can turn straw into gold. People who are deluded are a drain on everyone else on the team. Think about how this person is going to use up time and energy that could be better spent on another, more realistic person's goal achievement.

If the person merely has overly high goals due to immaturity, you need to break those goals down into smaller building blocks and create a plan for achievement. Think about what he really wants rather than what he says he wants. Later, as he slogs though the day-to-day hard work of getting to his goal, he will adjust his final destination to one that matches his capabilities. If he still holds on to truly unrealistic expectations of his life's path—and what he can do to meet it—it might then be time to cut him loose.

In all things, perfection is the enemy of the good. Stop letting the perfectionist inside of you sabotage your chances for progress. And if you find that your perfectionist is a colleague, business partner, or family member, you must stop giving so much weight to his or her unproductive perfectionism.

End Up with an Ally

I don't recall ever having had a discovery conversation with someone and not ending up with a more valued and trusted colleague and ally.

Once a leader has completed her conversations with all her team members and learned what's important to them, has a good idea of the journey they all want to be on, and knows where they want to end up, it's time to determine if she has everyone in the right positions. Frequently, armed with new information and insights, the leader will reshuffle the team to reflect not only skills and talents but ambitions and dreams as well.

Hear Them, Then Lead Them

Nobody summed up the goal of leadership communications better than the late David Foster Wallace: "A leader's real 'authority' is a power you voluntarily give him, and you grant him this authority not with resentment or resignation but happily; [because] it feels right. Deep down, you almost always like how a real leader makes you feel, the way you find yourself working harder and pushing yourself and thinking in ways you couldn't ever get to on your own. In other words, a real leader is somebody who can help us overcome the limitations of our own individual laziness and selfishness and weakness and fear and get us to do better things than we can get ourselves to do on our own."

Your title doesn't make people think you're worth following, and neither do your credentials. Taking classes in using your "command" voice or learning to project an executive presence won't help make your people "feel right" about you. No matter who you are, you'll inspire more, motivate better, engage your team, and get people to put their hearts into being faster and following through when you ask great questions, learn everyone's story, commit to helping them reach their potential, and connect the group's goals to where each individual wishes to end up. Nobody calls a person like that bossy; he or she is called a real leader.

FAST TASKS

- Make it a priority to schedule an hourlong discovery conversation with one of your employees each week, and follow the advice provided in this chapter. Really listen. By the time you've successfully completed a meeting with each of your direct reports, you'll know more about them, about who they really are and what they want to achieve, than you thought possible.

- The argument that having a discovery conversation with every worker in a huge company is impossible is not one that I accept. In a huge company the CEO might have eight to ten direct reports. Those are the people with whom she needs to have discovery conversations. If those ten direct reports have six to ten direct reports themselves, those senior managers need to have the conversation with their managers, who need to have them with their team, and so on. The process needs to be cascaded down through the company until the final shift supervisor has conducted discovery conversations with his teammates.

- Begin aligning people's responsibilities with what they want to achieve, not only with what you want them to achieve.

- Take time to enjoy the real pleasure you'll derive from helping people achieve what they want to achieve. Collectively, teams of people achieving what they want to achieve will make you faster and more successful.

CHAPTER SEVEN
Accountability

CREATE A *CULT* OF ENGAGEMENT AND CLARITY

When a company consistently outperforms the competition, we all want to know how it did it. Was its high performance due to some mind-blowing new strategy? Did leadership make a big bet on a trailblazing technology that paid off? Did a search committee find the perfect new leadership team? Or was it just luck?

Nitin Nohria, with his associates William Joyce and Bruce Roberson, researched those questions for their Evergreen Project. Among the many valuable conclusions from their study was this big discovery: What matters more than the choice of strategy, technology, or leadership style is "that whatever a company chooses to implement . . . they execute it *flawlessly*." Productivity, profitability, and growth are all the products of good fundamental management practices, a conclusion reaffirmed in 2014 by Nicholas

Bloom of Stanford and John Van Reenen of the London School of Economics with their meta research of ten thousand organizations across twenty countries. If you aim to be a winner instead of a loser or a climber instead of a stumbler, you need to execute better at every level.

At the same time the Evergreen Project identified the singular importance of thorough implementation, a research team from Ohio State's Fisher College of Business published another unique investigation, looking at the success rate of 356 implementation efforts over two decades. They watched executives working on the problems and opportunities in their organizations—recognizing gaps in performance, defining better outcomes, considering strategies, agreeing to a way forward, and then taking things from the conference-room strategy sessions to the front lines. The study found that half of all initiatives fail. According to Dr. Paul Nutt, who wrote about the findings in *Why Decisions Fail,* the initiatives examined in the study failed not because the strategy was bad or the need for a change went away but rather because "two-thirds of the time they used tactics prone to fail." That means that two out of every three implementations fail to use tactics that will generate enough follow-through to get any job done.

At the top of the list of the tactics prone to fail is implementing an initiative without first assigning clear accountability. Accountability has been proven time and time again to increase focus, drive, persistence, and productivity and lead to fast and thorough follow-through.

"Accountability for achieving clear, challenging goals improves business performance by 16 percent on average," Harvard- and Cornell-trained psychologist Dr. Edwin Locke concluded more than forty years ago. In 2013 Locke and Dr. Gary Latham examined another decade of scientific data (on top of the four hundred laboratory and field studies analyzed for their seminal book, *A Theory of Goal Setting and Task Performance*) and reconfirmed their original discovery. As long as an employee is committed, has the ability required to succeed, and is not torn by conflicting objectives, accountability will lead to significantly higher levels of task performance.

We've all seen accountability work miracles. It directs attention, focusing people toward completion of relevant actions and away from irrelevant tasks. It motivates individuals to search for new knowledge as well as to use all their current capabilities. Employees who are accountable to themselves, their teammates, their bosses, and the organization for specific, measurable goals learn more new things than those who feel less responsibility for specific outcomes. And when individual accountability is teamed with timely and relevant feedback from supervisors, especially feedback that shows how individual goals affect the outcomes of others, groups become more cooperative and coordinated, more likely to initiate problem-solving communication to overcome obstacles and achieve the group's goals on time.

Yet despite all the research, personal observations of the benefits, and our best intentions, accountability is still a major challenge for organizations.

Not Accountable? Watch Your Head

Several years ago a business-development manager at a technology company I knew faced this accountability challenge head-on.

"Sheesh," he wrote in an e-mail. "I don't know what to do. I was just told to pack my bags for Taipei next week. I'm supposed to demo a new product at an international wireless conference. So I asked the CEO, 'Which new product (since we have several) should I demo?'

He said, 'Ask the marketing director, it's his call.' I asked our CMO and he suggested I ask the CTO. When I asked the chief technology officer, he said, 'Not my call. Ask the VP of engineering.' That VP pointed his finger back at the CEO saying, 'This is part of his big new strategy so it's his call.' Round and round I went and at every stop I was told 'that other guy' should make the decision.

"What should I do?" he asked. "No one wants to take responsibility. No one wants to be accountable."

Ultimately he selected something to demo and presented it successfully in Taipei, because that's the kind of guy he is. Still, he was exasperated and baffled by the process. You know what he was thinking. *What the hell is wrong with these guys? They talk about accountability but sure don't want to take it. If I'm ever the boss,* I'll bet he said to himself, *one thing is for sure, we're not going to have any problems with everyone taking accountability.*

As fate would have it, that same business-development manager is now the CEO of a fast-growing, cloud-based technology provider. I called and reminded him of the e-mail he'd sent me eight years ago. "You're the boss now, and you've built your new business from the ground up," I said. "How have you solved that frustrating problem of getting people to take accountability?"

"It's not really solved," he said. "In fact, it's pretty much still the same story. CEO or not, it's incredibly hard to get everyone to take accountability. They're worried about being wrong, especially, I think, in technology and engineering, where there's always that one guy itching to crucify anyone who makes a mistake. Being CEO of a start-up has been like playing whack-a-mole: Try to hire the right kind of people, assign tasks, manage their mind-sets with rewards and praise, promote good peer chemistry, be sure I'm seen being accountable myself, and find the line between enough and too much accountability, and then double back to hiring more of the right people again. Everything I do is still not giving me a company where everyone takes accountability like I hoped."

He ended our conversation with a zinger. "Any chance you've got the answer?"

Sure, I thought jokingly, *just do like we've done for more than two thousand years and follow the tradition of the ancient Romans.* Whenever an arch was constructed in Rome, the engineer who designed it assumed accountability for his work in a most personal and unforgiving way. As the keystone was hoisted into place, he stood under the arch. If he didn't deliver as promised, he'd die when the keystone fell and hit him on the head.

CoBank's Strategy: So Much Better Than the Romans'

CoBank's CEO, Bob Engel, believes the answer to total accountability isn't to let keystones fall on the heads of people. Instead, he pinpoints greater executive engagement as the key to accountability. "Had that CEO and his top leaders [from the example above] been truly engaged in identifying what they were trying to accomplish," Engel says, "there wouldn't have been all the fingers pointed at someone else."

"Orders from on high don't get anyone following through in 2014," Engel says. "But anytime a CEO or top executive leader sits down across the table from those expected to execute and says, 'This is something that's really important to us. I'm going to entrust you and your division (or department or group) to be accountable. Let me tell you what I'm thinking, where we're trying to get, and let's have a discussion. What do we need to do from our end to execute?' You need total clarity but you don't get clarity sitting on your throne. You get clarity when you are engaged in the activity and you understand what's going on. You got to be out there. You got to be on the same page."

If you're thinking that that level of engagement sounds time-consuming and that few executives have enough hours in a day to work this way in a nanosecond culture, you're right. But Engel believes engagement is the only way leaders can make sure what's expected gets done. He makes it a priority. "It's 70 percent of my time," he says. "Fifty percent of my month is engagement with customers and 20 percent of my month I'm engaged with employees." Leadership's work isn't done in the conference room or around the CEO's desk in Engel's world; it's done where the real work is done. "The customers and the employees aren't in my office," he says.

Marshall Larsen's turnaround of Goodrich hinged on the same passion for engagement. When Larsen took charge, he had eighteen separate business units, each with its own P&L. While that kind of decentralization can be effective, at Goodrich it had fostered an attitude of "protecting one's turf" and "not coordinating with the other parts of the business." Larsen says, "This was simply wrong." So he undertook a massive directional overhaul, focusing on engagement. "We were relentless about having the executive team drilling deep into the company," he said. "We simply kept communicating our three big objectives with everyone: balanced growth (so that when one market sector was down, the negative impact to the company as a whole would be minimized), leveraging the enterprise (using the breadth and size of Goodrich as an advantage for every unit), and maximizing operational excellence (less waste, greater productivity), making certain that each executive's goals and plans were consistent with the big objectives. There were only twenty of us on the same page in the beginning. But finally we arrived at a place where if you asked anyone in the company what we were trying to achieve, you'd find everyone on the same page, all able to state our three big objectives."

If accountability can be difficult to master, how do successful leaders at high-speed companies get it started? By creating a cult of engagement and clarity.

Why a Cult?

Cults are defined as "groups of people having beliefs and practices regarded by others as strange." Strange is what many think when they hear about bosses like Stanley Bergman of Henry Schein who are on the road engaging with employees and customers twenty-six days out of every month. But isn't "strange" or "cultish" just a negative reaction to something unconventional that is also very uncomfortable (like sleeping in one's own bed only four days a month)?

Managers have been told for years to not micromanage people, to empower their staffs, and to let people work without bossing or breathing down their necks. Engagement can sound like it means "staying in their faces."

Some leaders have learned ways to engage people without harassing. Others haven't, and they turn the concept of *empowerment* into an excuse for abdicating responsibility and not being accountable for providing teams with all they need to be effective.

Let's not mince words. If your efforts to engage and to clarify goals and accountabilities stress your people out and are tagged as "micromanaging" or "bossy," either you've got the wrong team or you need a whole lot of work on your bedside manner. (Both, by the way, as Engel and Larsen will tell you, are your responsibility.)

CREATING AND CASCADING ACCOUNTABILITY

No business owner, CEO, or other leader desires to deliver conventional results. Everyone plans to outperform the competition. As quickly as they detail their desire for the achievement of unconventional, above-average results, though, they will fall back on conventional wisdom and do the same thing that everyone else is doing. If anything is strange, it's that logic.

You can reign—at least for a short while—over a terror-filled, highly accountable regime and demand accountability by forcing everyone to stand under a stone archway every morning while you lower the keystone into place. But you can't have the highly desired and pervasive sense of the right kind of accountability and maintain it without engagement and clarity.

People are ready and fully prepared to be fully accountable, if you provide them with an environment rich with good, competent leadership and high morale. Do these things consistently and eventually you'll have a cult of clarity and engagement and a high-speed company that outperforms the competition.

Prioritize Fanatically

If you want to be an *effective* executive, Peter Drucker advised in his famous book of the same name, do "first things first and second things not at all." Time is a leader's most limited resource, and according to Drucker that means managers have to really prioritize. I've seen that firsthand in interviewing many of the thousands of CEOs I've profiled over the years.

When Bill Zollars, the CEO who saved and transformed Yellow Freight into YRC Holdings, realized the company had to get out of the LTL (less than a truckload) freight business and into the logistics and solutions business in a big way, he spent a solid year of Mondays through Fridays traveling to the company's hundreds of freight depots meeting and engaging with tens of thousands of employees and drivers to get them on his side. When I asked him where he found the time to actually run the company, he said he did his CEO thing on Saturdays and Sundays.

During my time researching CoBank, I never got CEO Bob Engel on the telephone on a first attempt. Eventually I chided him a bit and asked if he was ever in the office. His response was typical Engel. "Every time I'm in my office," he said, "I look around and never see a customer or a member of our CoBank team." Engagement with CoBank's workforce and customers is Engel's priority, which is why he travels every month of the year to spend time with them. Eventually, everyone in the company saw what was important to Engel and began to emulate that behavior.

After my first interview with Dr. Jim Goodnight, chairman and CEO of SAS, the world's fourth-largest software firm, with a record twenty-nine straight years of organic double-digit growth behind it, I asked him how much time he actually spent managing and running the company. We had been speaking in a conference room; he motioned for me to follow him to his office. He pointed at a computer screen on his desk and said, "There's my dashboard; it tells me everything I need to know, from how much cash we have in the bank, how much we'll need to do everything we want to do, how many new customers we've added, how many we've renewed, how we're doing versus our sales and expense targets. As the captain of the ship, it's my job to steer us a little left if we're going too far to the right and a little to the right if we're veering too far to the left. How much time can that take?"

As the owner, manager, or CEO, you need to spend 70 percent of your time with your direct reports, members of your workforce, your customers, and your investors/shareholders. Anything less doesn't constitute engagement.

Hold on a minute, you might be thinking. *I can't spend that much time on engagement. I have a business to run as well.*

Actually, you do have that time to spend on engagement. The problem is, right now it's time that's probably being misspent on the wrong objectives.

"Average companies have 372 priorities they are tracking in their budgets; above average companies have just 21," wrote Sayan Chatterjee in his 2005 study "Core Objectives: Clarity in Designing Strategy." As a result of having seventeen times more stuff on their plates, average companies have poorer problem-solving communications, waste more precious time, and misallocate more expensive resources than the above-average company.

Culling that laundry list is not easy. You need to be a bulldog about quality guru Joseph Juran's 80/20 law. Juran wanted to help leaders separate the "vital few" from the "less useful many." His analysis concluded that 80 percent of results were generated by just 20 percent of actions. Almost eighty years after his initial research, however, it's clear organizations still haven't figured out how to apply this successfully. A recent study by Marakon Associates, an international strategic consulting firm, revealed that 95 percent of the leaders at 187 different billion-dollar-plus businesses felt their companies had no process and no discipline to help them focus and prioritize. As a result, 80 percent of their time was devoted to issues that affected a paltry 20 percent of their companies' long-term value. Despite spending twenty-one hours in meetings every week, "top leaders waste time discussing issues that have little to no direct impact," Marakon's Michael Mankins wrote, adding, "for example, one financial institution in the survey spent more time selecting the holiday card" than debating the plans for one of the bank's biggest new markets.

You need to constantly ask, "What's critical and what's not?" You need to search for the game changers, the activities that generate big results, and stop spending time on busywork that adds very little value. Your people look to you to tell them what's safe to ignore and what the priorities are. Yes, it can be hard to say certain tasks and activities your company has been doing for years are not important—it puts you at risk of being second-guessed. But as Bob Engel succinctly puts it, "I have the stripes. . . . The toughest jobs belong to me. If I'm not rigorous and disciplined about the things that are important, it just won't get done." Accountability and a cult of engagement start at the top.

Be Obsessive About Clarity

As the leader, it's your role to serve as the destination expert, constantly reminding everyone about the importance of his or her role in reaching the places the business is trying to reach, the good you're going to do, and how you're making the world a better place for your customers and your employees through your company's work.

Occasional one-off meetings, small groups, or even big annual conferences are not sufficient to achieve clarity. Nobody's words are such a powerful elixir that an occasional magical spoonful is good enough to get the job done. Like a daily vitamin regimen, a healthy eating program, or any other self-improvement project, it's an all-the-time commitment. Clarity takes obsessive practice and discipline.

Robert Greene, best-selling author of *Mastery,* argues persuasively that when it comes to mastering a skill, time is the magic ingredient. Assuming your practice proceeds at a steady level, over days and weeks certain elements of the skill become hardwired.

Slowly the entire skill becomes internalized. The mind is no longer mired in the details but can see the larger picture. It is a miraculous sensation, and practice will lead you to that point, no matter the talent level you are born with.

If your ambition is to create an enterprise where clarity—clear understanding, greater accuracy in all assessments, and freedom from ambiguity—is part of your culture of urgency and growth, this discipline must be practiced obsessively.

The best first step to achieving clarity is to demand that everyone in your company talk less and write more. Why's that?

"We have a tradition [in business] of managers getting together . . . talking in a conference room and then deciding things. The assumption is . . . pooled judgments provide an adequate basis for good decision-making. But that's a dangerous assumption," wrote NYU professor and organizational scientist Dr. William Starbuck in a 2003 article about the accuracy of managers' perceptions. Starbuck and his coauthor, Dr. John Mezias, concluded that "six out of ten managers" are very likely to be seriously out of touch with what's really going on. And when *out-of-touch* managers are asked questions they don't know the answers to, Starbuck's and Mezias's research shows, they are content to "fill the gaps with folklore." In other words, they repeat something they have heard or read in a magazine or try to string together enough jargon to sound knowledgeable.

A lot of executives know a lot less than they imagine, as you may have seen firsthand. The act of writing—whether on a possible solution to a problem, in response to a question, or about one's views on the current conditions inside or outside the business—forces individuals to think a matter through and be clear in their logic. Whenever you put pen to paper or fingers to keyboard, you understand, without being told, that others are going to read your thoughts and, based on what they see, judge you and your competency. Writing requires you to be more careful, thorough, and accurate. Further, when you write something down, you can see on the page the holes in your own logic, the haste of your conclusions, or, if your thinking is full of what my publisher likes to call "whipped cream," those long-winded stories and paragraphs of fluff where lots of words say very little.

Test this for yourself. Imagine someone asks you to explain what you mean by "good leadership." I'll bet you can start speaking on the spot. But if the listener starts taking notes as you answer or turns on a digital recorder, you'll ask for some time to do more homework and gather your thoughts, maybe write several drafts articulating what good leadership is instead of shooting from the lip.

The problem Starbuck and Mezias identified of six out of ten managers being seriously out of touch is something we can fix. Start with less talking and more writing.

Negotiate All Expectations

"How can I get engaged with my people and give them clarity when senior leadership is fuzzy and won't even give me clear direction?" asked a frustrated VP at a big international media company. Ever since a conglomerate acquired his business unit, he had felt stuck in the middle, wanting to meet stakeholders' expectations by engaging with his team to give them specific, measurable, and accountable goals but stymied by a barrage of conflicting, inconsistent, and incoherent directives from executives at the overseas headquarters.

In the last decade I've spoken with a lot of leaders who felt stuck in the middle at financial firms, manufacturing companies, high-tech start-ups, and other *Fortune* 500 organizations. "The most stressful part of my job is dealing with my boss's unclear expectations" is a common remark. As a result, I've watched them take one of these four ways forward:

- **Let all unclear directives from headquarters fall through the cracks.**

  "I just ignore everything I get from the head office until someone calls to yell at me," a branch manager told me. "That's the only way I can figure out what they really want. And honestly, 75 percent of the time I never hear another word."

  Turning a blind eye and ignoring directives is a terribly dysfunctional yet common practice in big companies. While I can understand the frustration and anger that could motivate such a response, this is a passive-aggressive form of sabotage and a bad strategy for getting headquarters to change.

- **Tell your boss, "That directive is too vague or is in conflict with what another executive said."**

  The chief learning officer at a technology company told a newly appointed EVP that he was frequently unclear, which made many of his directives hard for people to implement. The EVP responded, "I've spent a decade busting my butt to get clarity out of my bosses. Now it's someone else's turn to do the work."

  Since the bosses he had had over the last ten years had been incompetent, he was going to ensure that the same was true now for anyone who reported to him. Crap rolls downhill in this guy's world.

  Certainly not every newly promoted manager is that arrogant, but many are. Although I understand the motivation behind asking your boss to be more specific in his directives, there is a less confrontational way of getting clarity. I suggest the following third path, which I've seen work for getting clear expectations out of any boss.

- *Negotiate* **expectations.**

The most successful leaders have learned that they need to manage both up and down, leading both their bosses and their subordinates to be more effective. Often they must turn the vague, general, and conflicting goals of their bosses into specific, measurable, and agreed targets so they can give their people clear directions. It's a lot of work and requires strong communication skills.

First you need to see the situation from the boss's perspective. "I try not to be too judgmental," the chief of staff for a big financial company told me. "Maybe the boss is simply overwhelmed with other responsibilities and can't spend the time to make this thing clear. Or maybe they just aren't sure what they really want."

Next do some homework. "I'll put together a plan and ask for ten minutes to review my deliverables," she explained. "Then I'll talk them through it, asking, 'Does that sound right?' and 'Here's how I'm measuring it. Am I missing something?' It's an iterative process and I stay with it until I've got specific and measurable answers."

- **Read between the lines.**

Roger Vergé, the great French chef and mentor to many younger four-star chefs, respected natural intuition and instinct, knowing that great creativity lies in the heart and bears fruit when you have the courage to use your instincts. So he gave his students this unconventional cooking advice: "A recipe is not meant to be followed exactly. Let yourself be led by your palate and your tongue, your eyes and your heart. . . . Be guided by your love of food and then you will be able to cook."

That same advice helps you when you are trying to negotiate expectations. Your subconscious understanding of the pressures on your boss and your gut instincts about what's really a priority will help you understand what someone means without asking them to spell it out. Use your head and your heart to read between the lines. If you have a passion for your purpose and think about what you are hearing, you will be able to turn vague, general, or conflicting expectations into a clear direction.

Give Competent Feedback

Competent feedback in business, positive or negative, is incredibly rare. Most of the performance reviews we give are riddled with flaws like vague generalities, platitudes, and useless hindsight analysis. Let me paint you a picture.

There are twelve people in a conference room evenly divided into three teams. Each team is told to choose one person, blindfold him, and give him a four-inch foam ball. Next they are to point the blindfolded teammate in the right direction and tell him to toss the ball into a trash can–sized receptacle that is exactly ten feet away.

Each team gets ten shots and the goal is to make the most on-target throws. However, the rules are different for each team. Group one is prohibited from saying anything when handing the blindfolded teammate the ball for all ten shots. Only after all ten shots can they give him any feedback, such as "Your first shot went too far and the second was too short" and so on.

Group two is allowed to talk each time they hand the ball for another shot at the receptacle but must restrict their comments to "You're doing a good job" or "Keep trying; we believe in you," offering nothing specific but lots of encouragement.

Group three has no restrictions. They can do whatever comes naturally. During their round, they can give the blindfolded teammate details about how and where the last lob missed and offer advice about force, trajectory, and direction. They can even take time to answer questions from the blindfolded teammate.

Now, as you imagine that scene, answer the following questions:

- At the end of the first round of ten tries, which team would likely have the best results?
- Would it change if you gave the three teams the same rules but a second round of ten tries?
- Which blindfolded team member would be the most enthusiastic about being handed the ball for that second round?

This exercise echoes performance feedback at most companies. The first group represents our year-end-performance-review school of feedback. All the advice is given so far after the fact that it's not very helpful. The second group symbolizes the high self-esteem school of feedback. It makes the giver feel like he's doing something of value but to the receiver it's just vague niceties but totally unhelpful. The third group represents the only "good" feedback. They gave commentary that was timely and specific and therefore useful and motivating.

Fifty-eight percent of workers told consulting firm Mercer that their supervisors did not give them regular feedback. In this case, regular means timely as well as consistent. All year long people need to adjust, tune, get refreshed, and put things in their proper perspective. Critiques can't really help if you get them in one big dose with the year-end performance review. It's just common sense. It takes at least 440 pounds of protein, carbs, fat, and fiber to sustain the average person for a year, but no one would think they could save time by eating all that at one sitting. To sustain life, food needs to be consumed daily. The same is true of feedback.

Even more important than regularity is that critiques be helpful, useful, and knowledgeable.

I asked a roomful of mangers in a breakout session after a keynote speech, "What are the qualities that you want from a leader?" After reciting a long list of all the things they probably had heard in other workshops or read in magazines—confidence, charisma, integrity, communication skills, persistence, a vision, blah, blah, blah—I asked each to reconsider, using this criterion: "If you needed to cross a minefield and someone said, 'Hey, everybody, go this way,' would it matter to you if they had charisma, a vision, confidence, or any of that other stuff?"

"Not really," I heard. "The most important thing would be for them to *know* the right way to get out of the minefield."

That's what people really want from feedback; not inspiration or motivation but specifics from someone who has taken the time to learn which path is best.

Me Too

Two years ago I personally went through a situation that illustrates what happens when you fail to provide engagement and clarity.

Each summer my family moves from California to our place in northern Michigan for several months. I had recently hired a new housekeeper for our home in California, and because I believe in a policy of no layoffs, I asked that she and her helper continue working there, even though there wouldn't be much regular work for them to do while we were away. Since she knew the house better than we did and had always showed a lot of initiative, I thought she would use the extra time to clean closets, reorganize pots, pans, and utensils, and give some elbow grease to anything else that needed attention.

When we returned home a few months later, the place was clean, but a quick inspection revealed that not one of the things I'd hoped she'd do had been done. I felt let down and betrayed. We'd been generous, kept her employed all summer, and had received the bare minimum in return. A few hours later I had my epiphany.

The problem wasn't with the housekeeper; the problem was with me. When I pointed an accusatory finger at her, there were three fingers pointed directly back at me. I hadn't engaged with her, hadn't been clear about expectations, and in turn she hadn't fulfilled them. I was the problem; I'd failed to provide clarity, and without it there can't and won't be accountability.

The next year the housekeeper and I came to an agreement about the special projects she'd undertake and the things she'd get done, and we laid it out on a week-by-week basis. When we walked in the door after our time away, everything on the list had been done to perfection. Her project list was on the kitchen counter, with each project crossed out with a smiley face and a date next to it, and the refrigerator was fully stocked. When I called to thank her, her pride at being acknowledged bubbled through the phone line.

I share that story of my personal failure instead of a business example for a simple reason. Even though I'm the guy who has screened more than 200,000 companies, studied 55,000 of them, interviewed more than 11,000 of the world's best business leaders, and written six books on the subject . . . I still screwed up. And I bet you have too, even though you're as smart as you are!

While accountability is foremost in your mind and mine, it's not top of mind for most people. So when we fail to provide the clarity that leads to accountability, imagine what's going on a rung or two below us on the ladder. Accountability requires that the leader build a cult of engagement and clarity, a group of people having beliefs and practices regarded by others as strange. Imagine how great that will be.

FAST TASKS

- Spend a minimum of 70 percent of your time engaged with customers or staffers.
- When discussing and assigning tasks to your direct reports, stop talking about general outcomes and instead discuss and negotiate the specific outcomes expected. Members of your direct team will catch on very quickly and begin doing the same with their direct reports. Keep it up, don't relent, and it will cascade throughout the company.
- Embrace Peter Drucker's motto for effective executives: "First things first and second things not at all." It will help you prioritize those things that truly require your attention.
- Instead of feeding your direct reports 440 pounds of protein, carbs, fat, and fiber in one meal (the annual

review), initiate a weekly or biweekly program. This will force you to get totally engaged.

- Conduct an initiatives census and come up with the total number of tasks being worked on by the company. Working with your direct reports, reduce the number to twenty or fewer. Better yet, recall what Marshall Larsen, former CEO of Goodrich, did when he slashed that number to three:

"We simply kept communicating our three big objectives with everyone: balanced growth (so that when one market sector was down, the negative impact to the company as a whole would be minimized), leveraging the enterprise (using the breadth and size of Goodrich as an advantage for every unit), and maximizing operational excellence (less waste, greater productivity), making certain that each executive's goals and plans were consistent with the big objectives."

CHAPTER EIGHT
Prosperity

KEEPING FAST PEOPLE BY YOUR SIDE

I love finding the "road to Damascus" stories in business—those significant incidents when lightning strikes, Saul becomes Paul, and people discover ideas that change their world in a big way.

Charles F. O'Reilly, founder of O'Reilly Auto Parts, had his "road to Damascus" moment back when he was seventy-two years old. It came when O'Reilly's longtime employer had planned to let him go as the manager of a local auto parts store in Springfield, Missouri, on the recommendation of a consultant, who'd said, "Fire the old man and transfer his son [who was the store's assistant manager] to St. Louis." Instead of heading meekly into retirement, O'Reilly rented a building down the street and opened up his own store. All twelve of his employees from the auto parts store followed

him to the new shop, and each made a financial investment—
whether a few hundred dollars or the modest proceeds of a mort-
gage on their home—in the business.

By 1961 O'Reilly was about to open the first branch of his auto
parts store in Springfield. Sales were up substantially from $700,000
in revenues during the first year, but so were expenses, and O'Reilly's main financial partner, a shortsighted investor from New York,
told him they needed to start taking money out for the stockholders.
By "stockholders" the investor mostly meant himself, because he
owned 49 percent of the company, although O'Reilly and the others who had put money in would also receive a share of the profits.

O'Reilly realized that if the investor(s) started taking out all
the profits from the business, the company wouldn't have the resources to hire more people and expand and therefore wouldn't be
able to grow. Even though he was on the precipice of his late seven-
ties, O'Reilly envisioned big opportunities ahead for the company
and was resolved to do everything he could to make growth happen. Further, he believed in his heart that putting his personal
prosperity first wasn't the mark of good leadership. So instead of
putting his investors first, O'Reilly went to his local bank and asked
for a loan of $200,000 so he could buy out the New York investor.

O'Reilly's grandson, David O'Reilly, the current chairman of
the company, remembers how frightening it was for his grandfather
and his father to go to the bank and borrow the money ($200,000
in 1961 is about $1.6 million in 2014). They'd always believed that
having to borrow money was an admission of failure. But the pair
risked everything they had—putting the *long-term* interests of the
business and their current and future employees ahead of their own—
and personally guaranteed the loan to buy out the moneyman.

Over the next two decades, O'Reilly Automotive grew fast.
Five stores became fifty, then a hundred, then five hundred, seven

hundred, and one thousand stores. In 2014, as the company closed in on $7 billion in annual revenue, it was operating in 4,200 locations, with clear runway ahead for more growth in the future. Revenues had also grown steadily, with double-digit increases in fifty-five out of the past fifty-seven years.

Whether it was through instruction or intuition, Charlie O'Reilly set the tone for his company by following the path of one of the ancient world's greatest leaders. In 540 BC the Persian king Cyrus the Elder, who quickly expanded the first Persian empire and brought innovations like postal service, roadways, and a common language to fifty million people, learned a better way to motivate than the carrot and stick. "Leaders can always compel obedience," Cyrus told his son, "through the threat of punishment or the seduction of gifts. But great leaders look out for their followers better than they look out for themselves and always do so before taking care of their own interests. Who would not want to follow the leader who put the interests of the follower ahead of his own?" his father asked him.

David O'Reilly has vivid memories of those who followed the leader who put others' interests ahead of his own. "I didn't know what I was witnessing at the time, but everybody, and I mean everybody, that worked with my grandfather and father treated the company like their own and did whatever they needed to do to find a part for a customer, up to and including driving halfway across the state if they needed to and delivering parts on Sundays if the customer needed something."

Succeeding in the auto parts business is very hard work. There's no protected territory, no built-in competitive advantage. Anyone can open a store across the street and match your prices. Retail means long hours, demanding customers, big money tied up in inventory, and low margins. Growth can be accomplished only through a fierce sense of determination and grit.

But because O'Reilly made his people's growth and prosperity more important than his own welfare, his workers doubled down on their commitment to the company. Armed with a reason for doing good, with a strong set of guiding principles and systematization in place, and fueled by a fierce sense of urgency, the company took off and has never looked back. It says something that the company has tweaked but never changed its business plan and model.

Companies committed to the financial prosperity of their workforce have five traits in common. They are committed to

- consistent growth;
- quick advancement of talented team members;
- a culture of abundance;
- a fierce sense of fairness;
- security for team members.

Consistent Growth

If you fail to grow, you'll fail to create prosperity for your workers. The two are inseparable. Growth, therefore, must always be the top priority in a high-speed company. As I learned recently from a roomful of high-tech professionals and one very candid CEO, there is no alternative.

"How many of you would like to earn more money?" I asked the five hundred technical managers, divisional executives, and senior directors in front of me as I began my speech.

Every hand went high in agreement.

"Now," I said, "raise your hand again if you'd like a promotion or additional responsibilities."

Once again, every hand in the room went up.

"Last," I asked, "tell me when you'd like that to happen: sooner or later?"

"Sooner," they yelled, in one voice that echoed through the ballroom.

I stole a look at the CEO. He was frowning, his lips were tight, and his eyes went down to his pad of paper. He started scribbling notes.

Uh-oh, he looks irritated, I thought. As soon as the speech was finished, I walked up to him and asked, "Did I say something wrong?"

"No," he said, shaking his head. "But what my people told you is going to keep me awake at night."

"I'm not sure what you mean," I said.

"Every person said they want to get ahead and they want prosperity," he said, "and I know it's up to me to make it happen." Then he added a very sobering thought: "If we can't grow and grow fast enough to get these people those 'better tomorrows' you talked about, they'll leave and I'll be up the creek without a paddle."

The challenge of growing, combined with the fact that only a minute percentage of businesses have cracked the code on sustained growth, has spurred a lot of leaders to scramble for some other approach to prosperity, an alternative strategy to try when growth is just *too hard.*

Recently John Chambers, the CEO of Cisco, a man I really

admire, tried a new narrative in an interview with *Fortune* magazine. He was asked to explain his company's recent lackluster top-line growth. He responded that the 2000s had been years of growth but that going forward the company's priority was to improve profitability based on *existing* revenue levels. Anytime you hear a CEO downplaying the outlook for top-line growth but making big promises about improving profitability, you should be very concerned (and indeed, Cisco announced layoffs a short time later). A CEO who is trying to sell that story is really saying that he or she hasn't been able to figure out how to grow the business and is going to start cutting expenses to keep all the short-term Wall Street analysts happy. We've seen it too may times before: Announce big layoffs and watch the stock go up a bit, announce plant closures and watch it bump up some more, eventually the best executives start leaving . . . and you know the rest of the story. If the CEO cannot figure out how to grow the company, it's time for a change, because without growth there's no prosperity for anyone in the organization.

As chairman and CEO of Arrow Electronics, Mike Long also presides over a worldwide technology components and solutions provider. Arrow has grown its revenues by 50 percent in the past five years (despite an unsettled European market suffering a prolonged recession), and Long believes there is no other narrative, no alternative to growth.

I asked him one day if he ever took a break from focusing on growth. He looked at me incredulously and answered emphatically, "No!"

"Your shareholders are that demanding?" I asked.

He looked at me as if I'd just fallen off a turnip truck, then visibly went into teaching mode. "Companies that always act first and foremost in the short-term interests of their shareholders frequently do stupid things like lay people off, slash product offerings, and shutter facilities," he explained. "The reason a CEO must be resolutely committed to growth isn't for the benefit of the shareholders but for the benefit of the workforce."

What did he mean?

"Every single one of the 16,500 people who work for Arrow wants to earn more money and eventually get promoted. They all want to do better," he said. "But if the company isn't growing, there won't be any money for raises and there won't be any promotions unless someone retires, dies, or gets thrown under a bus, and eventually the good people will leave. If they leave they'll either join my competitors or become my new competition.

"My number one responsibility as a leader is to make certain we're growing fast enough that no one will ever feel that they have to leave Arrow in order to improve their lot in life," Long said. "As soon as they've mastered a set of skills and want to further improve themselves, I'd better have something new to challenge and reward them or I'll find myself spending all my time trying to replace people. When you're able to find, keep, and grow the right people, that's when you're able to find, keep, and grow the right customers, and that's when your shareholders end up being very happy."

Greg Henslee, CEO of O'Reilly, agrees wholeheartedly with Mike Long. "This year we'll open another two hundred stores and three huge distribution centers, so we have many hundreds of management and leadership jobs to fill and loads of opportunity for people," he says. O'Reilly's commitment to keeping fast people on board clearly hasn't changed since Charlie was in charge.

According to Henslee, growth keeps his team motivated and exponentially increases the speed at which they can operate. "Can you imagine what would happen if we ever announced we were done growing and were just going to stick with the stores we already have? It would be disastrous. Our shareholders would be disappointed, but the effect on our people would be crippling," he says. "A company that isn't growing and where people are only able to count on employee turnover in order to get a promotion and do better financially isn't a good company to work for."

Advancement

Lots of people leave their jobs for a better opportunity. According to 2014 research reported in *Forbes,* an average of 2.5 million people wave good-bye to their boss each month in the United States. That's an astounding thirty million jobs a year out of a total of 120 million jobs, which equates to an average employee turnover of almost 25 percent. Even during the depths of the great recession, the number of people leaving their jobs each year averaged more than nineteen million. And the average American worker spends only between four and five years in a job before leaving in search of a better opportunity. It's no surprise that it's so difficult for most companies to gain any traction; they're like hamsters going round and round on a wheel inside a cage.

Turnover and employee churn are the enemies of cultures of speed and growth. Vast amounts of time and resources are spent on screening, hiring, training, and trying to bring up to speed replacement workers. Those precious resources would be better invested in achieving organic growth, making lots of small bets, buying or acquiring other companies, and making certain nobody feels they need to leave the company to improve their lot in life.

I'm not overstating this. While bad bosses are still cited as a main reason for leaving a job, almost every other conceivable reason can be directly connected to employees wanting a better future. When people are bored and unchallenged at work, they'll walk away. When there aren't enough opportunities to use and improve their skills and abilities, they'll eventually take a hike. When a job has no meaning, people will jettison it. When there's no recognition and no clear way forward, they will walk. When their financial future doesn't look promising, they'll say sayonara sooner rather than later.

According to the global consulting company Mercer, in the United States 74 percent of heads of HR say that their employees are aware of advancement opportunities within their companies, but when the employees at the same companies are quizzed, fewer than 25 percent of them say they are aware of any chance to advance—one more example of how what we believe isn't always fact.

The best way to make certain that the entire workforce is aware of opportunities for advancement within a company is by practicing what you preach. If you truly have a policy of promoting from within, do it and make each promotion a cause for celebration. Until leaders understand that growth isn't an option but a requirement and make it a guiding principle of their organization, they will continue to be plagued by people jumping ship in search of greater opportunity.

Abundance, Not Scarcity

Every leader I've ever met and interviewed has one of two easily discernible points of view on the world. Either they come from a position of abundance and believe there's enough to go around for everyone or they come from a position of scarcity, don't believe there's enough to go around, and are determined to get as much as they can as quickly as they can.

Leaders who don't believe there's enough to go around become takers. Eventually they will be surrounded by others who share their negative view of the world. These are not good ingredients for building a fast company.

I first interviewed David O'Reilly ten years ago for my book *Think Big, Act Small,* when he was still serving as the company's CEO. At the time, it was hard for me to imagine that what the company had achieved in the 1980s and 1990s could be continued in the future. O'Reilly discounted my concerns. "For many years we had a saying that the customer was the king at O'Reilly's," he said, "and while we really believe and practice that, I always let our new hires in on a secret. Our secret is that while we truly do treat our customers like kings, we actually take care of our own people first, value them above everything else, and exist to provide them an opportunity to do well. That's how we're able to deliver superlative customer service."

Greg Henslee, O'Reilly's current CEO, is celebrating his thirtieth anniversary with the company. He says his greatest thrill continues to be helping the company create opportunities for its 67,000 team members, continuing Charlie's legacy. Henslee knows firsthand how prosperity planning works at O'Reilly.

"During college I worked for a car dealership as a service writer taking service orders for the dealership's repair shop, and then went to work in the auto-repair business for Montgomery Ward. The repair shop bought parts from O'Reilly," says Henslee. "When Ward's made changes that I thought treated customers unfairly, I decided to leave and applied for a job with O'Reilly."

Like almost everyone else, Henslee started working behind the counter, selling parts. In a short time he was promoted to assistant manager, and he hoped to become a store manager in time. One day he got word that Charlie O'Reilly wanted to see him; when he went to meet with him, Charlie offered Henslee a district manager role. A few years after that, when the company decided to convert from a paper-based inventory-control system to computers,

Henslee got the nod to run that sector, even though he knew very little about computers. When that task was successfully completed, he was made the VP of store operations, then copresident in 1999 and CEO in 2005. He reached that level thanks to O'Reilly's abundance mind-set, and he's not the only one in the company who has been able to prosper that way.

"The same opportunities that I've had have been enjoyed by thousands of people at the company," says Henslee. "This is retail, and starting wages average eight to ten dollars an hour. We hire people for an entry-level job, give them all the tools and direction they need, ask them to do the best they can, and if we see that they can get the work done, have high potential, and want to be part of our culture, we'll start promoting them and giving them more and more responsibility and opportunity."

At O'Reilly, all full-time employees become shareholders within six months and receive a generous matching 401(k) and a solid benefits package. The favorite stories told by David O'Reilly, Greg Henslee, and other members of the leadership team are about people who joined the company working behind the counter and who, years later, between their retirement accounts and the stock options they'd been given or purchased, retired with millions.

"We truly care about the total well-being of all our team members, and that includes having work/life balance, time off with their families, the opportunity to advance as far and fast as they want and are able, and being compensated for the value they create," Henslee said.

Fairness

In the closing pages of *Animal Farm,* the pigs inform all the other animals, "All animals are equal, but some animals are more equal than others." Sadly, that seems to be the way it is at many companies, where only a few at the top share in the financial performance of the business and there's no pathway to prosperity for the majority of the workforce.

In contrast, high-speed companies with cultures of urgency and growth are much more egalitarian in nature.

There's nothing wrong with CEOs and senior leaders being justly and highly compensated for the economic value they create. What isn't right is when a few folks at the top have looted the coffers and there's nothing left to compensate everyone else in the organization for the value they've created and provide them with a path to further prosperity as well.

At O'Reilly they bend over backward to be fair. Everyone, including the CEO, receives the same package of benefits. As Greg Henslee explains it, "Ours is a culture of treating everyone fairly, including our team members, customers, our vendors and suppliers. My benefits package as the CEO is the same as everyone else in the company, nothing more and nothing less. For example, I get the same amount of vacation time as everyone else working here, and my benefits are the same as any other team member's."

"Everyone here is trying to do the same thing," says Henslee, "and that's to provide better customer service than our competitors. We're all working together and share the same values of teamwork, honesty, hard work, trust, and respect, so why shouldn't everyone receive the same package of benefits? If you claim respect as one of your values, you have to begin by being respectful."

Prosperity planning does a lot toward keeping team members feeling like a valuable part of the organization, which induces them to work hard and fast as well. At O'Reilly such planning includes allowing employees to spend 5 percent of each paycheck on company stock at a 15 percent discount and a 6 percent match on the company's 401(k) program. As people are promoted, they also receive stock options.

Henslee knows that O'Reilly's attitude and emphasis on fairness differ from that of many other companies. In 2008 O'Reilly purchased another company and was shocked at how the acquisition's leaders treated themselves differently from the workers. "It was amazing to see how the leadership viewed themselves as better than and separate from the workers," he says. "They thought they deserved better benefits, better lifestyles, more vacation time, and all the other things that the workers are unable to give themselves.

"Once you start separating yourself from the workforce," Henslee says, "it starts building on itself, and before you know it, instead of being inches apart, you're miles apart. I wouldn't want anyone in our company to feel like I'm not working at least as hard as I'd expect anyone else to work. Receiving the same benefits just seems logical, fair, and fundamental."

The practice of fairness is one reason Henslee believes O'Reilly has been successful for so long and is still growing. "Show me a company where the executives at the top have their own culture of leisure and entitlement, and I'll show you a company that's going to have big trouble down the road."

Security

In recent years, knowing you'll even have a job tomorrow has become an important part of prosperity planning for people. At the same time, it's also become standard operating procedure at most companies to fire someone when he proves himself incapable of doing a job. What Greg Henslee and O'Reilly do when that happens flies in the face of conventional wisdom. They don't terminate people lightly.

"If someone steals or does something illegal, we fire them," says Henslee, "but we very seldom fire people for any other reasons. People are simply too valuable to us."

Prosperity planning at O'Reilly means quickly promoting and rewarding workers as soon as it's become obvious they've bought into and become part of the culture and have mastered their jobs. "Once people show us, 'Hey, I can do this job,' we say, 'Well, maybe they can do this other job too,' and we promote them and give it a try."

What if those promotions don't work out, though? What if O'Reilly promotes an achieving team member too soon and finds itself with a good person in the wrong role?

"We really don't make a lot of mistakes from a promotion stand-point, but when we do, what happens is that we've made it okay for people to come to us and say, 'I think I've bitten off more than I can chew. I think I'd like to have an opportunity again sometime, but for now I'd like to step back for a while.'"

That's certainly not common practice at most organizations— and you might be surprised to learn that this kind of flexibility and security works at high-speed companies, where the priority is growth and quick adjustment. But it's worked for O'Reilly and has allowed it to keep valuable team members by helping them grow into new roles instead of forcing a fit.

A common situation, according to Henslee, is that O'Reilly promotes a great salesperson to a supervisory or management role. While the person knows the inventory and has great customer-service skills, he or she might not have the skills yet to manage people, navigate more complex relationships with our installer customers, or understand financial matters.

"You'd never want to lose someone like that [a great salesperson]," says Henslee, "so we've built a great way of bringing them back into a position called an Installer Service Specialist that allows them to be compensated very well and stay with the company. The position has actually become an incredibly important job. These people have the customer relationships that are the glue that holds the stores together; they have tenure, know parts, and have been involved in management, so they know all the details of how a store operates. It's become a great way of retaining people and letting them continue to do well."

CREATING AND CASCADING PROSPERITY

There is a direct link between creating prosperity for fast people and keeping those same fast people by your side. It's something that you either see or are probably not open to seeing. Companies that provide the right people challenging work, constant opportunities for advancement, fair compensation that acknowledges the value they've created, a solid benefits package that doesn't favor only a few at the top, stock or shadow stock options and/or a chance of buying in and becoming an owner (and with it the possibility of achieving true long-term financial prosperity), and thanks for a job well done will attract and keep the right workers.

Henslee sees it. "We motivate through opportunity to get ahead through expansion," he said. "That has been our strategy for fifty-plus years."

Mike Long of Arrow sees it. He says, "No one who works for Arrow should ever feel they have to leave and join another company in order to be challenged or to better themselves financially. It's my responsibility to make certain that we're staying ahead of people's need to be challenged, master new skills, and provide for their families."

Jim Ryan of Grainger sees it. "We benefit seven ways. Lower turnover, higher engagement, more successful recruiting, more durable customer relationships, a greater share of people's discretionary time, more active ambassadors, and ultimately better operating results. We have a great responsibility to create opportunity, build for the long term while delivering on the near-term commitments promised to our investors—not always an easy balance to strike, but regardless of what's going on in the economy we will always find a way to invest in growth and create prosperity for our people. It's proven to be a great move for our company."

Leaders like Henslee, Long, and Ryan have ingrained prosperity into their organizations. But over many years we've seen that even the best intentions and plans are too often wasted because leaders don't have the buy-in and a road map for specific participation from all associates. And that is not because prosperity doesn't appeal to everyone. Rather, there is often a mistaken sense of entitlement attached to the desire for prosperity.

Leaders need a gut check that ensures their people are prepared to match all the efforts that the company is making to provide prosperity and invest enough to make prosperity likely.

It's not a hard thing to do. You can get that thorough gut check by asking a few questions about what each associate has invested in the past in order to improve their lives and what they could bring to the table now in order to create a better tomorrow for themselves and their families.

What Would *You* Invest?

I've got an image stuck in my head, put there by Ichigo Umehara, the former CEO of Asia's Pan Pacific Hotels and Resorts chain. We were talking about that sense of entitlement I had seen in the baby-boom generation and he agreed it was an all-too-common attitude. Then he told me of a cartoon he'd seen of a man seated at a table with his mouth open so wide you could see all the way back to his uvula. The picture's caption was "Ancient proverb: A man must sit in a chair with his mouth open for a very long time before a roast duck will fly in."

The point Umehara was making is a critical lesson for any leader who wants to plan prosperity for his people. Leaders can seize opportunities for growth and they can be generous with resources, but team members can't expect to just sit there and have prosperity fly into their laps. They have to make and continue to make an investment in themselves.

My parents' generation understood this. They went to night school to pick up the knowledge and credentials to advance in their careers. They purchased their own work tools, came in to the shop on weekends, stayed late, picked up extra assignments, and constantly invested their time, money, and effort toward gaining skills and proving their worth. They routinely deferred fun and vacations and all other immediate gratification to invest in their better tomorrows.

Somewhere in the last four decades, we've lost their instinctive understanding that every person must invest to get ahead. It's not that people today have never invested; anyone who has excelled in sports, the arts, science, mathematics, scouting, volunteerism, or extracurriculars of any kind has experienced the link between investing time, money, grit, a positive attitude, and willingness to learn and achieving their goals. But society has fed them the message that simply putting in your time or gaining tenure means you deserve greater rewards. That message sticks. It's a fatal misconception and one you need to correct when you plan for prosperity, both your company's and that of the people who work with you.

I'm sure you've heard someone say, "I'm going to be very disappointed if I don't get this promotion or raise." I'll never forget how one of my favorite mentors responded to me when I said those words. "I hear you," he said. "So tell me, what's *your* plan to avoid being disappointed? I mean, it's your responsibility too, isn't it? How are you going to make it impossible for them to not choose you for the promotion? What value have you added that makes it a no-brainer to give you that raise?" When I didn't have a good answer, he told me nicely but firmly that I'd better find an answer. It's a lesson I learned and I'm forever grateful for it.

Now it is your turn to prepare people to do their part in creating prosperity. It's only fair. Pay it forward.

The best way to accomplish the gut check is by continuing your discovery conversation, as outlined in chapter 6. There are just a few additional questions you should ask, and they fall under five main starting points.

1. What would you like to be earning in the next twelve months? In twenty-four months? In five years?

   Why? What would you do with that money?
   What kind of percentage income increase would that take?
   Have you ever accomplished a similar increase in earnings?
   Tell me what you did to earn that increase.

2. What new responsibilities or professional advancement would you like to achieve in the next two years and in five years?

   Have you ever been promoted like that in the past?
   Tell me what you did to earn that kind of advancement.
   What new skills did you master?
   What accomplishments preceded the promotion?

3. What do you believe are your top three skills that would qualify you for the kind of promotion you would like?

Is there anything you would like to be able to do better?

What kind of time, money, and effort would you invest to reach these goals? Be specific.

Would you invest hours beyond the normal workweek to reach your goals? Tell me about a time when you made that kind of investment.

If the plan to achieve your goals required a personal financial investment, could you make it? Tell me about a time when you spent a significant amount of money gaining new skills or on technology tools that helped your career.

Have you ever persevered in something difficult and succeeded? Tell me about it.

Finding out what advancement and prosperity is worth to each team member is crucial.

If what he or she is willing to invest is not sufficient, the leader must either negotiate the associate's expectations of prosperity down or negotiate his or her investment up. And if there is no way to make this plan work . . . you're better off knowing that now.

Two concluding questions and you're ready to craft their road map.

4. What do you need from me?
5. How can I help you?

What you are looking for here is for your direct report to help you construct a road that includes your participation as his leader. Does he need more feedback from you? If yes, discuss what you need from him in order to provide good feedback, like a regular time to meet or an openness to hearing something uncomfortable about his performance. He may need help prioritizing his projects or some gentle nagging when he's off track. This is a time for frank, confidential conversations. You want the best for your team members and you need to know what they need and what they will respond to.

I suggest you close this conversation with one more question: "If I do that and you get to your goals, what would you do for me to say thanks?" Yes, that's right, I expect a payback: a letter of thanks, some extra help when I need it to hit the group's goals, telling others on the team how he's succeeded and how they can too—some small services that show he recognizes I've been helpful.

I ask that last question for several reasons. First, I need all the help I can get to lead others to their full potential. If I am able to turn every success into a mentor, it makes my life easier. Second, I'm motivated by knowing I've been of value. Leaders don't hear that enough. As my friend from Pan Pacific Hotels explained, "When the leader's work is done, his people say, 'Look, we did it all ourselves.'"

FAST TASKS

- Answer the following question: "Am I as excited and enthusiastic about the prosperity of people who work for me as I am about my own?" If the answer is no, be prepared to spend a disproportionate amount of time searching for, hiring, and training new workers to replace those who are leaving or will leave.
- Recognize that growth is intentional and make it one of your company's guiding principles. Growth is not impossible (if you follow the advice in this book). Like speed, the only things that get in the way of growth

are the speed bumps and roadblocks organizations place in front of them. Without growth, there won't be prosperity for anyone.

- Make it clear that you're prepared to invest in the prosperity planning of your workforce and that, in return, there is an expectation that people will invest in their future prosperity as well. It won't happen simply by virtue of showing up or by tenure. Your team members need to be as fully committed to their prosperity and advancement as the company is.

- Like O'Reilly, develop a "fall back" program so that when people are promoted and are having difficulty, there's a way to step back to another role, continue to grow in the company, and work up from there. The alternative is to lose everything your team members have to offer the company and its customers, just because they weren't the right fit at a given time—but might be in the future.

CHAPTER NINE
Stewardship

THE FINAL PIECE OF THE PUZZLE

In doing research for this book, I became preoccupied with finding the one trait shared by all the people who lead high-speed companies, successfully create cultures of urgency and growth, and do it long enough to make what they do worthy of further study. I made many lists of possible candidates for this one key element, yet that single trait eluded me. There always seemed to be an exception to any rule.

One day an answer came to me so suddenly that I actually had to pull off the freeway and park to explore it further. "There are really only two types of people in the world," the voice inside me said, "Those who go through life feeling *It's mostly about me,* and those who go through life feeling *It's mostly about others.*"

It was like a whack upside the head.

The people who lead the fastest and best-performing companies don't see the world's problems, opportunities, rewards, and costs through the lens of what these things mean to them, I realized. They understand that true happiness and satisfaction come when we focus on others. They are, at heart, caregivers who see their purpose as being the best stewards of the resources, both tangible and intangible, that have been entrusted to them and making sure that all assets are used efficiently, effectively, and profitably.

That single shared trait I'd been looking for was *stewardship*. It was also the essential last piece of the puzzle for creating urgency and growth in a nanosecond culture.

Stewards come in all shapes, sizes, genders, orientations, and nationalities but share the understanding that their work and their effort are mostly about other people: inspiring them, celebrating them, serving them, and genuinely liking them. They also have a humble understanding that their mission is to improve the well-being of five different groups:

- Workers
- Customers
- Vendors and suppliers
- Investors and owners
- Society

Living a life focused mostly on others changes everything about a person. Stewards are less tied up by their own egos, making them less stubborn and narrow-minded and more adaptable and flexible, both important attributes for quick action in a complex world. They are less opportunistic in their dealings (opportunism, as defined by the Nobel Prize–winning economist Oliver Williamson, being "self-interest seeking with guile," "guile" meaning willingness to use deceit, cunning, or schemes to achieve what's best for one alone).

Stewards want trust from all five groups. They know the profound and proven economic value of being trusted, believing that cost savings and greater organizational velocity come with being trustworthy. Stewards are also more optimistic, seeing possibilities where others see dead ends, good where others see bad, and the power of personal responsibility where others seek justifications or someone else to blame.

Stewards avoid "carrot and stick" management principles. As Mel Haught, recently retired CEO of Pella Corporation (one of the nation's premier window manufacturers) and a very good steward, told me, "We forget that the same people we're with at work go home on the weekend and build a new church, remodel a schoolroom, help a neighbor fix their car, or organize local fund-raising efforts, all on their own." He believes it is a steward's responsibility to "unleash and focus those same motivations in their work."

That's not to say that stewards are never demanding business leaders. Nor is every steward a Goody Two-Shoes without any faults or foibles. Walt Disney said, "We don't make movies to make money. We make money to make movies." That's the attitude of a steward. However, Disney could also be as difficult and demanding as his detractors make him out to be.

Back when Disney needed to show the New York City moneymen what this place called Disneyland would look like if he could get them to invest, he called on his friend, the artist Herb Ryman (of *Dumbo* and *Fantasia* fame). "Herbie," he said to his friend, "I know it's Saturday, but my brother has to take drawings back to New York on Monday to show them what Disneyland will look like."

"I'm not going to do anything in two days," Ryman shot back. "You've got a lot of nerve calling me on a Saturday morning, asking me to come up with something in two days. Nobody in the world can do it. It will embarrass you and me. I don't want anything to do with it!"

Yet two hours later Ryman was hard at work, and by Sunday night, Disney had a colorful set of drawings with a detailed vision of the park to show the investors. Do you think the typical boss can inspire people to pull rabbits out of a hat and do the impossible? Absolutely not. Disney was able to ask Ryman and his other employees for extraordinary feats because he had already established his stewardship with the people who mattered most.

Stewards Are Made, Not Born

When I meet someone running a high-speed company whom I identify as a good steward, I always look for the untold story, the people and incidents that shaped that person's uncommon perspective. I want to know if that person was a steward from birth or if certain events and people made him or her into that good steward. Bob Engel is typical.

"I only had one hero . . . my dad, a great guy who landed in Normandy on D-day plus one," CoBank's CEO says, beaming with pride. "My dad was as hard a worker as I've ever met, but most of all he was good. He had compassion for others like I've never seen. He became my role model. But when I was just seventeen, my dad suffered a massive stroke. The doctors told us, 'Your dad probably won't live, and if by some miracle he does, he'll finish his life a vegetable.'

"My dream had been to become a doctor and play Division 1 football at Notre Dame," Engel says, "but with my dad's brain severely injured, I went to my mom and said, 'I can't go to Notre Dame now; I've got to run Dad's business.' And I enrolled in a local college, learned accounting and taxes pretty quickly, and began running his accounting business."

Engel put his dreams on hold to be the family's steward. And like all the great stewards I've met, he took his tragic turn of events and created his first mighty purpose. He recalls, "I decided if learning business and working on financials is what I had to do, I'd better love it and put everything I had into it." Engel's story shows that stewards are definitely made and not born. As children, we're all focused on ourselves and see the world selfishly, through the lens of our own self-interest. As we get older and see examples from our family, teachers, and other adults around us, many of us start questioning whether fulfillment and happiness come when we focus solely on ourselves or when we focus on doing things that bring happiness and fulfillment to others. Stewards decide that for them, the greatest happiness comes when they are doing for others.

But in my discovery conversations with scores of leaders who are great stewards, I learned something quite surprising. Great stewards are never made by a single person or event, and when I inquired about the other role models who inspired stewardship, there was almost always the story of some seriously flawed antihero who seemed to firm up the resolve of the future steward. "I'll never do what they did," is the common refrain I hear from stewards telling me of some awful boss or authority figure and his or her long-lasting influence.

For example, early in his career Engel was working for Marine Midland (which eventually became HSBC) and attended his first senior leaders' meeting. As he tells it, the CEO asked each of the group heads onstage with him to give a summary of his or her business unit's performance during the previous year. "Each stood up, talked about how well their business unit had done, how they'd exceeded their plan and each had a great story. When they were done," Engel says, "the CEO stood up, lowered the head on his six-foot-six-inch frame, and announced the company has just had one of its worst years ever.

"I was stunned," recalls Engel. "I went to school to be an accountant and I know that one plus one equals two and if you add a series of positive numbers, like one plus two plus three and so on, that you'll eventually end up with a positive number, not a negative, money-losing number. All those supposed leaders *had gamed the system* and won and *probably got big bonuses* while the bank lost. That day I promised myself that for me it would never be about individual wins but the entire team winning. What kind of person would enjoy winning if their team loses?"

It's "monkey see, monkey do" for many executives as they rise through the ranks. "My boss never made things clear for me," I've heard more than one CEO say. "I went to the school of hard knocks. I had to learn to figure it out. Adversity was good for me. So I'm not going to coddle my people," and then, inevitably, they add some dinosaur-speak like "What doesn't kill you will make you stronger."

A steward learns what *not* to do from that bad boss. Stewards don't repeat the bad behavior of a flawed father, mother, teacher, or boss. They learn from the missteps of others and do what will help their people, even if that wasn't done for them.

Stewards Pull a High-Speed Company Together

A steward's purpose in a high-speed company is to cultivate assets and grow them successfully for the benefit of employees, customers, investors, suppliers, and society. Assets are both tangible things like equipment, patents, and customers and intangible things like how-to knowledge, brand reputation, and great relationships. Stewards look to improve such assets through thoughtful action, sowing the right seeds, adding necessary nutrients to the environment, removing things that inhibit growth, reducing resistance, and generally advancing the potential growth of the firm so they can provide a good return on investment for those same five groups.

The previous eight chapters are a road map for achieving a steward's purpose. When you connect doing good with your goal of delivering a good return on investment, make the "shalls" and "shall nots" of your strategy clear to all, anticipate and neutralize the immutable law of suckage, make your company a transparent, trustworthy entity, create a cult of clarity and engagement that systematizes everything and communicates by listening, and promote prosperity for all, you will create an unbeatable culture of urgency and growth.

But the work of a steward doesn't stop with launching the culture. Many great companies had the right culture and then lost it: AOL, RadioShack, Bear Stearns, Sears Roebuck, Andersen Consulting, and General Motors, among many more. Once you create a high-speed-company culture, it's vital that you do everything to keep the culture healthy through thick and thin.

That's a huge challenge. We understand how difficult it is because of all the best-intentioned, highly capable leaders we've watched create a lot of terrific momentum and then lose it, never to recover.

CREATING AND CASCADING STEWARDSHIP

"A culture is a living, breathing thing," Greg Henslee of O'Reilly said. "It's the bloodstream that keeps our organization growing. Without it O'Reilly Automotive and our 67,000 people would become just another retail company going through the motions. And if that happened, then we'd stop growing and we'd die."

Looking at your business as a biological organism instead of an inanimate mechanism is critical for maintaining momentum with a culture of urgency and growth. Your company is not a machine that just needs new cogs and gears to perform faster and better; it lives and breathes with a heart that beats and a soul that needs to be nourished.

As a steward, how do you keep the culture you've created strong and thriving? I found the answer in a very unlikely place.

Every summer members of the Keweenaw Bay Indian Community host their annual summer powwow on the shores of Lake Superior in northern Michigan. The multiday event is attended by hundreds of the hosting Ojibwa Indians, members of other tribes from around the nation, and thousands of spectators. As the powwow begins, scores of loud drums and chanting musicians welcome the attendees, outfitted in their colorful native garb, to the festive Grand Entrance Parade. There's an abundance of tribal food, trails in the forest are crowded with vendors selling their handmade wares, and music and games and stories go on until long after dark.

I was walking through the forest at the powwow when I came across an Indian chief in full regalia sitting on a blanket surrounded by many spellbound children. I stood nearby and listened in on his story. Soon I realized his riveting and poignant story was a lesson in keeping and growing the right culture.

"There's a vicious fight inside of me," the chief said. "It's a fight between two powerful wolves. One is the wolf of arrogance, envy, greed, fear, and fury. The other is the wolf of generosity, humility, truth, love, and gratitude."

The children sat very still, listening with their full attention, picturing this war inside the chief. "The same fight going on inside of me will one day be inside of you, my children," he said, moving closer and looking each child in the eyes.

Finally one boy, frightened by the thought of a vicious struggle, wondered what he could do when the fight began in him. "Chief," he asked, "which wolf will win the fight?"

The chief whispered, "The one you feed, my son. The victor is always the wolf you feed."

Just as it illuminated the right path for children struggling between good and bad, the chief's story also has applications for leadership. Keeping a culture strong and thriving requires cutting the unhealthy stuff from your diet, starving that bad wolf while you bring a bounty of the best and feed the good wolf.

Stewards Starve the Wolf of Negativity, Cynicism, and Bureaucracy

No leader sets out to let his or her company become dysfunctional. But it happens a lot. Dysfunction grows fastest in companies where leaders allow negativity, cynicism, or bureaucracy to be born and thrive.

Negativity

Watching *Hell's Kitchen, MasterChef, or Kitchen Nightmares,* you've seen Gordon Ramsay scream, berate, and even throw plates at contestants who don't live up to his expectations. It's a shtick, I'm sure (I hope), but it reinforces a dangerous misconception, that all high-performing organizations are led by prima donnas who are so passionate that they simply can't stop themselves from spewing negativity at anyone who's not doing what's expected.

One of the fastest-growing restaurant groups in America has thought long and hard about what it means to subject everyone in their organization to prima-donna negativity in order to achieve high quality. To the leaders of the Union Square Hospitality Group, negativity was wrong on many levels, which is why they've built their culture to eliminate the negativity. The inspiration behind their breakthrough success strategy wasn't a leadership book or a Sunday sermon. It was one exhausted executive's late-night encounter with room service.

Richard Coraine, then the COO and now a senior partner of Union Square Hospitality Group, arrived at his hotel after midnight, thanks to air-traffic delays and baggage problems at the Atlanta airport. He got to his room, tired and hungry, plopped on his bed, and immediately dialed room service.

"I'd like a bowl of chicken soup and some crackers," he said.

To his surprise, the woman from room service didn't just take his order. She thought that a guest calling so late for chicken soup and sounding like he was half asleep might not be feeling well, so she went off the company script. "Are you feeling okay?" she asked, concerned. "Because that's an order I get when somebody isn't feeling well."

"No, no, I'm fine," replied Coraine, clearing his throat. "I just got off a plane and I have an early-morning business meeting. I'm hungry and I'm tired, but I'm fine."

"Well, I'm glad you're not ill. But still I'm going to put a note on this order to get everything to you quickly so you can have your soup and get to sleep fast," she said.

Her level of concern not only made Coraine's stay at the hotel that much better, it inspired him to think about how easily this server's great hospitality could be derailed.

"I'll bet that young lady makes about eight or nine dollars an hour," Coraine told me. "Yet she did more to build that hotel's hospitality brand than a million-dollar TV campaign. But had the night chef seen her note and yelled at her for promising a rush or reported her to management and she got reprimanded for improvising instead of following procedures, that would have killed her initiative."

That realization inspired Coraine to create the "no skunking" rule for all the leadership at the Union Square Hospitality Group.

"Skunking is what we call it when someone sprays negativity over another staffer," he explained. "We avoid unthinking acts of negativity (even if unintentional) and take special care to increase awareness of negativity among our leaders." USHG knows that the courage to use your head and your heart is hard to muster. One critical comment can extinguish it.

The no-skunking, no-negativity rule helped USHG quickly become a high-speed company, growing from one restaurant to scores of brands and locations, earning Michelin praise, four-star reviews, and a "#1 restaurant in New York City" distinction from Zagat nine times in a row. The company has more than three thousand associates and, according to the ratings group Technomic, annual revenues are now approaching $500 million. It has become a high-speed company thanks, in no small part, to eliminating negativity from its recipe.

Cynicism

Cynics conclude that everyone is just like them: selfish and dishonest. They are distrustful of human nature and question people's motives. Cynics know, as Oscar Wilde said, "the price of everything and the value of nothing." There's no way to build a sustainable high-speed company based on a culture that feeds cynicism. But cynicism is so rampant I felt it was beyond my control until I heard the best sermon ever.

The Reverend Bob Brohm didn't walk to the pulpit that Sunday, as was his routine when it was time for his homily, but instead chose to stand in front of the congregation at Shepherd of the Hills Lutheran Church. He gazed out, took a deep breath, and said, "I'd like you to raise your hand if you believe that we as a people are becoming more cynical."

There was an awkward pause as people nervously glanced at one another, not used to being asked to raise their hands in church and probably fearful (at least in my case) that they might get called on if theirs was the only hand raised. Eventually, as people considered the question, they started putting their hands in the air, and in short order every hand was up.

"This morning I'd like to talk about cynicism," the pastor said, "and why we've become so cynical and what we can do about it."

"How many of you have ever had overly high expectations?" he asked. "Please raise your hands."

It didn't take long before every hand was in the air. After all, who hasn't been unrealistic and dreamed the impossible would happen?

"What happens when you have overly high expectations?" he asked. "You get *disappointed.*

"Does being disappointed because of our overly high expectations stop us from doing it again in the future? Of course it doesn't," he said, answering his own question. "But perhaps the next time, instead of becoming disappointed, we start becoming a little *disillusioned.*"

"Does having been disappointed and becoming a bit disillusioned prevent us from ever having overly high expectations again?" he asked the congregation. Everyone started nodding.

"The next time we get let down by our own overly high expectations, we move from disappointment and disillusionment to a feeling of *despair,*" he said. "When it happens again we start feeling *deceived* and our view of everyone and everything around us starts to turn *cynical*. My friends, the path to cynicism is plain to see. It's paved with overly high expectations and our typical human reaction to feeling let down again and again."

Stewards who protect the culture in high-speed, urgent enterprises don't let disappointment mutate into feelings of disillusionment, despair, and being deceived. They don't allow cynicism to grow. When a company's workforce is fed a constant diet of either overly high expectations or cynicism, its members will eventually become cynical as well. It's the responsibility of a steward to make certain that promises made are promises kept and cynicism is never fed to the culture.

Bureaucracy

In 2014 Microsoft announced the largest layoffs in its thirty-nine-year history, reporting that it would be letting about eighteen thousand people go. The majority would be professional and factory jobs related to Microsoft's acquisition of Nokia, with another six thousand expected to be cut from the ranks of established Microsoft staff and executives.

In announcing the layoffs, new CEO Satya Nadella called them "difficult but necessary. We need to become more agile and move faster." For that reason, the *Los Angeles Times* and others have anticipated that the six thousand staff and executives laid off would be part of the Microsoft bureaucracy.

Many analysts weighed in with their opinion that, while the cuts would be painful, the company needed them to become "leaner and meaner." I feel sorry for those affected by any layoff, but for the life of me I can't imagine anything "painful" or "mean" about shedding bureaucracy. Analysts really don't get it!

The *Encyclopedia of Political Theory* defines bureaucracy as "characterized by hierarchy, fixed rules, impersonal relationships, rigid adherence to procedures, and highly specialized roles in overseeing or policing." Bureaucrats do not make a tangible contribution to the good purpose of the firm, nor do they have an accountable role in finding or growing customers. They are administrators, the process police who create drag instead of velocity.

Bureaucracy is the number one "misguided" element that slows us down and wrecks our momentum. If Microsoft has the grit and guts—it'll take a lot of both—to cut bureaucracy, these layoffs can actually show good stewardship.

Just how onerous bureaucracies can be was made vividly clear for me the year before 2008's great recession in a tiny airport in West Virginia.

Once a year the American Society of Automotive Engineers holds a gathering of the nation's top automotive executives at the Greenbrier resort in West Virginia. Hundreds of CEOs, VPs, and other senior leaders from all the major automobile companies come together to talk about their industry, and in 2007 I was there to deliver the opening keynote address. Following the speech I was scheduled to catch a commuter flight from Greenbrier Valley Airport.

Knowing there'd be no food on the flight, I decided to grab something to eat in the airport's small restaurant, which was jammed with people. As I was waiting for a table, a man walked up and said, "Great speech this morning. I really enjoyed it very much and learned a lot." He introduced himself as Mark Templin, at the time the VP of Toyota's Scion brand and now group VP and general manager of Lexus North America. He asked if he could join me for a quick lunch, during which time we talked about the key points of my speech.

When we'd finished our lunch and were walking to our gate, he stopped to look out a long set of windows overlooking the runways. He motioned me to join him and said, "Look out there and tell me what you see." Before I could even look, he added, "Even though you got a standing ovation this morning and everyone told you they loved your speech, what you see on the tarmac are the reasons that not one person who was in the room this morning will ever do anything with the information you presented."

I looked out the windows. All I saw was row after row of private jets, far more than a small airport like Greenbrier should have parked on their tarmac.

"You know who those airplanes belong to?" asked Templin. I shook my head. "They all belong to the big car companies," he said. I asked him why they needed so many private jets and why the attendees couldn't have flown together to reduce costs, and his response was priceless and prescient. "The reason you climb the ladder at the big three is to eventually get your own private jet. Being able to fly alone is a status symbol at the big three, and it's their huge bureaucracies that will be their undoing one day."

A year later, without bankruptcies and huge government bailouts, both GM and Chrysler and their bloated bureaucracies would have closed their doors for good. As further proof that unless you're willing to learn from the past you're doomed to repeat it, both companies are profitable again, their bureaucracies as big as ever and, in the case of GM, so bloated that a faulty ignition switch responsible for at least thirty deaths and hundreds of thousands of serious injuries was never brought to the attention of the senior leadership team. While everyone wishes GM's new CEO, Mary Barra, the best, it's fair to point out that GM has proven that bureaucracy can even lead to death.

Count them. Unless your company has five or fewer layers between the lowliest and the highest people on the totem pole, you have a bureaucratic mess that will eventually render you incapable of being a fast company able to act with urgency. And anything you're doing to feed your culture more bureaucracy will one day be your undoing.

Stewards Feed the Wolf of Adaptability and Respect

As the tribal elder taught the children, there are two wolves inside each of us—and inside each organization. If the first step is to starve the wolf you don't want to win, the second is to feed the good wolf so it can flourish. Cultures of urgency and growth thrive as you cultivate adaptability and respect.

Adaptability

In 1992 when Harvard's Earl Sasser, John Kotter, and James Heskett published the links they had found between strong cultures and superior business performance, they barely made a ripple. Business leaders were mostly fat and happy, still benefiting from the previous decade of strong economic growth. Detroit's "big three" ruled auto manufacturing, the big three TV networks ruled the audience ratings, Starbucks was a pint-sized company, Microsoft was three years away from making the *Fortune* 500, and Tim Berners-Lee's first World Wide Web page could be seen only on a NeXT computer. Cultures of anything—especially urgency and growth—were not a business priority.

Buried deep in that original research was an incredible finding that would clearly identify the kind of company culture that would grow faster and profit more as the world became increasingly complex and quick moving. They originally thought that an organization's performance was related to the strength of its culture. But Sasser and his colleagues wrote that they "found to our dismay, there was no measurable relationship." Then they compared strong cultures that outperformed the average with strong cultures that were below average. "The clear differentiator between high and low performing firms, all with a strong culture, was the ability of each firm to adapt," they wrote. The message was clear: Strong cultures don't win as consistently as adaptable ones.

Grainger believes that. Jim Ryan, Grainger CEO, sees that firsthand. "You have to adapt to customers. Anything they buy from us they can go down the street and buy from someone else," he says. "We live and die based on our ability to deliver better and exceed expectations. But expectations are a moving target. The needs of customers change, behavior changes, and the competitive environment changes. The challenge is to keep the cornerstones of our culture strong while we flex, adapt, and grow.

"What that requires, I found," Ryan continued, "is for everyone to understand what has to change and what has to stay the same. The five keys to success that have defined us for eighty-seven years need to stay—service, honesty, integrity, hard work, and service to the community are what must stay. But beyond those keys to success we have to adapt. For example, we've changed from a company where we primarily promote from within to a company that values different perspectives, different voices, different backgrounds, and different industries. We've deliberately developed a mix of people who have grown up in this business with other people from different places and other experiences. We look for the common ground—work ethic, honesty, and the ability not just to appreciate the customer but also to embrace them—and we hire those characteristics. Then we all pull together."

Organizations that install cultural devices for feeding the spirit of adaptability not only greatly improve their chances of sustaining high performance over time but also increase their chances of successful transitions from one leader to another. Ryan does it by welcoming new voices with different ideas while also helping his longtime employees stay open to fresh thinking.

Rigid leaders end up with brittle organizations. Adaptable leaders end up with flexible teams in companies that can turn on a dime.

Respect

Managers struggle to show enough respect to their teams. That's not because they are all coldhearted or clueless bureaucrats by nature. Often when one is leading a team in volatile, fast-changing situations, trying to keep missteps to a minimum and get the job done on time, it makes sense to give people strict directives and demand unquestioned compliance. At least it *seems* to make sense.

Behavioral experts studying failures, especially tragedies occurring in difficult environments, conclude that strict directives and demands for unquestioned compliance send a message that you don't respect the individual's ability to make good decisions on his or her own. Professor Michael Roberto of Harvard explained in his 2002 analysis "High Stakes Decision Making: The Lessons of Mount Everest" how strict directives and expectations for unquestioning obedience were partly to blame for the 1996 catastrophe on Mt. Everest in which eight people died. Professor Jody Hoffer Gittell, who wrote in 2011 about the role of respect in acute-care medical decisions, concludes, "Respect . . . reinforces an inclination to coordinate . . . and increases the problem-solving nature of communications." If you want teams to coordinate, solve their own problems, and give critical feedback freely and immediately, you need to feed the wolf of respect.

Showing respect starts with what you believe is going on inside other people's heads. Do you believe most people are trustworthy? Do they like responsibility or do they shirk it? Do you think most people prefer to work rather than sit idle? Do they want meaning from their daily work, or is it just about a paycheck for most of them? Do they like to learn, or is that just too hard? Finally, do you believe most people will resist or embrace adapting and bettering themselves?

Your beliefs influence how you communicate, what you read between the lines, and the respect or lack of respect that is implied when you communicate freely or cut off any input.

You're already further along in understanding how to show more respect if you've read this far. If you live up to your purpose, you show respect. If you give people clear guiding principles and boundaries, avoiding micromanagement, you show them respect. Listening shows respect, as do practicing transparency and trust and sharing strategy and knowledge. When you let the best idea win and give credit to others with excitement and enthusiasm, respect soars.

To fully show respect as a steward, however, you also must stop everything in your company that shows disrespect.

Tom Kelley is the best-selling author of *Creative Confidence, The Art of Innovation,* and *The Ten Faces of Innovation,* as well as a partner at the renowned design and innovation consultancy IDEO. In its early ramp-up stages, IDEO was always avoiding actions and attitudes that disrespected the individual.

"I have a friend and she went to work for a big law firm," Kelley says. "She decided to pin up a very nice poster in her office . . . really more of a work of art. Away from her desk for an hour, she saw someone had removed the poster. When she asked about it, the office manager said curtly, 'First of all, we don't use pushpins here. Secondly, any *art* must be approved in advance by the *art committee*.'"

Kelley believes removing that woman's poster and admonishing her as if she were some disobedient peon was a sign of great disrespect. The move announced to the organization, "We don't trust you to use good judgment, and therefore we're keeping our eyes on you." Treating people with respect, Kelley said, is about "not getting all *rulebound*."

Paul Nunes, executive director of high-performance research at Accenture and author of *Jumping the S-Curve: How to Get on Top, and Stay There*, told me, "It's the difference between having a culture of honor or a culture of laws. Talented people and high-performance businesses want a culture of honor." Reliability in a nanosecond world, Nunes's research shows, comes from respect and honor.

Marshall Larsen, the CEO who pulled stalling aerospace giant Goodrich out of its descent and made it soar, saw how an emphasis on respecting teams to do the right thing makes the difference. Larsen's conclusion is succinct: "Don't make rules for the 5 percent of people who don't comply." Larsen's is the opposite approach to that taken by most big companies and bureaucracies, like the art-removing law firm. They look for an exception and use that as motivation to add another page to the process manual. Larsen, who trained at West Point and learned combat leadership as a U.S. Army Ranger, thinks that approach utter nonsense and a waste of resources. Instead, he says, look to those who do comply with your values and principles—with the big picture, not on the unimportant stuff. "We work hard to get those 5 percent who won't comply out of the organization," Larsen said. "Actually, we found that our strong culture and the good people will eventually push them out."

A Visionary, an Authority, and, Most of All, a Storyteller

The answer of how stewards feed their culture was another lesson I learned from a highly unlikely place for management strategy: Kurt Vonnegut's novel *Bluebeard*. In the book the painter Rabo Karabekian is listening as his neighbor, Paul Slazinger, tells him about his new project, titled *The Only Way to Have a Successful Revolution in Any Field of Human Activity.*

> . . . Most people cannot open their minds to new ideas unless a mind opening team with a peculiar membership goes to work on them. Otherwise, life will go on exactly as before, no matter how painful, unrealistic, unjust, ludicrous, or downright dumb that life may be.
>
> The team must consist of three sorts of specialists. . . .
>
> . . . An authentic genius—a person capable of having seemingly good ideas not in general circulation. "A genius working alone is invariably ignored as a lunatic."
>
> The second sort of specialist . . . a highly intelligent citizen in good standing who understands and admires the fresh ideas of the genius and who testifies that the genius is far from mad. "A person like that . . . can only yearn out loud for changes but fail to say what their shapes should be."
>
> The third sort . . . is a person who can explain anything, no matter how complicated, to the satisfaction of most people no matter how stupid or pig-headed they may be. "He will say almost

anything to be interesting and exciting. . . . Working
alone . . . he would be regarded as being as full of
shit as a Christmas turkey."

". . . If you can't get a cast like that together,
you can forget changing anything in a great big
way," he [Slazinger] says.

When I first encountered the preceding words, I realized that
in many ways they were an almost perfect distillation of my life's
work doing research, writing, and teaching. Consider their enor-
mity and implication. They say that for anything of any value to
happen you need three things: a visionary who imagines or sees it,
an authority with credibility who gives it the stamp of approval,
and a storyteller capable of getting followers on board.

Those three roles sum up the story of HP's early years, the incredible early success enjoyed by Apple, Microsoft, and Google, and
an almost endless list of companies that acted with urgency,
achieved remarkable success, and were truly high-speed companies.
When some of them stumbled, it was because they lost the visionary, the authority figure, or the storyteller, because they started
taking their success for granted, or because the person at the top
became delusional and thought he or she was capable of playing all
three roles, which is seldom the case. Very few people are capable
of being a visionary, an authority, and a compelling storyteller. Authentic stewards are able to honestly assess their true capabilities
and have no problem sharing some of the limelight with someone
who performs one of those roles better than they do.

If you're capable of creating a purpose and a set of guiding
principles and values, you will be a visionary. If you systematize
everything, listen, avoid the immutable law of suckage, and create
cults of engagement and clarity, you will be an authority. But being

a visionary and an authority won't feed the followers you need to truly become a high-speed organization committed to urgency and growth. You need to either become an accomplished storyteller or find and appoint a masterful storyteller to create the lore that will nourish the wolf of urgency and growth.

Who Is It About and What Am I Prepared to Do?

Stewards accept the responsibility of making everything better for the five constituencies they serve (their workers, their customers, their vendors and suppliers, their shareholders or owners, and society). They're not wrapped up in everything being about them but instead in helping others achieve their full potential.

Cultures will become what they're fed. Good stewards never feed their cultures negativity, cynicism, or bureaucracy but instead a steady diet of adaptability, respect, urgency, hustle, and the stories needed to fuel the culture and keep it alive, vibrant, and relevant.

It's time for you to ask yourself two important questions. The answers will reveal not only the real you but also how ready you are to lead a high-speed company that will be able to withstand the tests of the marketplace and of time. There are things your husband, wife, or partner, your friends and coworkers and family members don't know about you. But you know the whole truth about yourself. Looking as deep inside your soul as possible and being brutally honest, ask yourself the following:

1. Is everything mostly about you or mostly about others?

2. Are you ready to be a good steward in everything you do?

If you decide that you're prepared to be a good steward in all you do and everything you undertake, the only Fast Task you need to do is to pick one time every day to briefly renew the promise you've made to yourself and say, "I will be a good steward in all that I do."

Here's to lasting and meaningful speed, urgency, and growth in a nanosecond culture!

ACKNOWLEDGMENTS

Laurence Haughton and I were at the start of a long journey that would take us from San Francisco to Narita, Japan, where we'd connect to a long flight to Singapore, then board a small boat for a long ride to an Indonesian island we'd never heard of, where we would be leading a three-day retreat for a group of Australian and New Zealand business owners, CEOs, and their senior leaders. Door to door the trip would take thirty-four hours and we'd be repeating the trip homeward bound in a few days. We'd made an almost identical trip two weeks earlier.

Before the airplane was even off the ground, Haughton looked at me with a big grin and asked, "And exactly why are we doing this again?" His question sparked a conversation that lasted the entire trip and didn't end until we stepped off the boat, exhausted, in Indonesia.

We weren't making the trip to see a new part of the world; we'd made the Asia run many times. We weren't doing it to collect frequent-flyer points and we certainly weren't doing it because we enjoyed being away from our families. After hours of nonstop conversation, punctuated by an occasional hour of fitful sleep, we finally answered the question "Why *are* we doing this?"

We were doing what we did because it's a thrill to help lead people and companies to their full potential. As long as I've been doing this work, I can honestly say that I've never lost the thrill. In fact, it only intensifies with time. And I'm blessed to be surrounded by a group of people who understand why I do what I do, help me in more ways than you can imagine, and are all directly responsible for this book.

Here are the important people who made this book possible:

I've worked and collaborated with Laurence Haughton for more than twenty years. He's been a VP at my company, fellow consultant on scores of projects worldwide, coauthor, writing partner, head researcher, and someone who knows me better than I do. He's brilliant. When we're working together we speak and text scores of times daily, and each communication is like a breath of fresh air. I can't imagine creating, researching, and writing a book without his collaboration and friendship.

Next there's Adrian Zackheim and his terrific team at Penguin Random House's Portfolio imprint. Adrian is the most accomplished business and leadership publisher in the business and I'm honored to be published by him. This is my seventh book for him and I hope there will be many more. Adrian's team at Portfolio includes Will Weisser, the head of marketing, and Jacquelynn Burke, in charge of publicity for this book. As always, I count on my literary agent, Alan Nevins of the Renaissance Agency in Los Angeles, for his invaluable advice and guidance.

Acknowledgments

I'm fortunate to have worked with many very good editors for previous books but have never worked with anyone like Natalie Horbachevsky. Without a doubt she's the most talented, tough, challenging, questioning, and exacting person I've ever met. When she sent back the first draft of the introduction (the first thing I write and continually revise while writing a book), there were so many notations, notes, and scribbles that it looked like a brood of drunken chickens had marched over it. I remember thinking, *Uh-oh, this is going to be very long and hard,* but after thinking about it for about thirty seconds I decided to give myself to this late-twentysomething, highly accomplished Boston College graduate. I reasoned that her far younger set of eyes could only make the book more relevant and appealing to a group of readers who might otherwise not get me. She'd also shake me up a bit, which, according to people close to me, is always a good thing. I ended up being thrilled and a far better researcher and writer because of our association. I hope Natalie edits all my future books. She has an incredible future ahead of her.

My assistant and speaking manager is Caryn Shehi. She manages every aspect of my calendar and business life. She is amazingly organized and efficient and naturally understands the need to always exceed the client's expectations. She's a wonderful person, very funny, and not above bringing me down to earth with an occasional "Stop whining" when the going on the road gets really difficult.

Mark Powell, my travel agent, always gets me where I need to be despite itineraries that would confound most mortals. He's superb. The people who drive me to the airport, pick me up, and get me where I need to be include Ruben, Whitt, and Khalid in California, Solomon in Denver, Jesse Schramm in northern Michigan, and Erol Hafizbegovic in Florida. I've never missed a flight, research interview, or speech because of these great guys.

My technology needs are handled by William Deane, an extremely talented and patient soul who, over the years, has taken me from dial-up to the cloud and understands my desire to be an early adopter but also realizes I'm saddled with having been born on the wrong side of the digital divide. He's helped and bailed me out and saved more chapters and manuscripts from being lost than you can imagine. In addition, there are two amazing women, Karen DeLise and Leslie Marcotte, at the Word Gallery in Corte Madera, California, who over the years have spent many thousands of hours listening to, transcribing, and organizing all the interviews that go into my books. They are the best.

My Web site, jason-jennings.com, is filled with information about my books and is masterfully handled by Marc Moellinger, another brilliant and creative force in my life. My podcast, *The Game Changers,* based on my books, is produced and hosted by Dale Dixon, who challenges me with questions on a weekly basis and who possesses the unique ability to listen to something very complex and repeat it in a way that makes it easy to understand and accessible to everyone.

For more than a dozen years my family's financial and administrative needs have been handled by Christopher DiSalvio, kind of our major domo, who keeps the books, accounts for every nickel, and also takes care of myriad other needs. CPA Steve Stenberg takes care of our finances and Bruce Ritter, our financial planner for more than twenty years, is a best friend and has been the inspiration for two of my books.

Most of this book was written and edited at our summer place, Timber Rock Shore, on a lake in Michigan's Upper Peninsula. It's hard to explain the inspiration provided by an early-morning hike and encountering a mama bear and her cubs, a moose, a pair of soaring eagles, or a doe and her spotted fawn. This very special place has been cared for and managed year round since we built it by Gene and Judy Nagle, who have become special friends and again a source of inspiration. Judy is one of the best questioners I've ever met, and when interviewing CEOs I frequently ask myself, "WWJA?" "What would Judy ask?" Starting in 2015, the Nagles will retire to winters in Florida and be replaced by Jay and Nicki Killoran, the new stewards of TRS.

For intellectual and physical stimulation and health, I study and speak Spanish with Ana Baradello, play the viola with Zamil Sadiq, and work out at the gym with my trainer, Jeff Marth. Inevitably, the questions, prodding, and curiosity of these people help form my books; each sees my ideas and books through a different lens and offers a unique and invaluable perspective.

Without the speaking agents who book my speeches a lot fewer books would get sold and read, and I am grateful for their support. Here are the agents I've been privileged to work with during the past year: Rainey Foster, Lisa Raines, Steve Bagshaw, Tony Berardo, Ryan Foltz, Kathleen French, and Tara Newman at Leading Authorities in Washington, DC; Gary McManis, Jay Callahan, John Truran, and Kelly Skibbie of Keppler Speakers in Arlington, Virginia; Bob Thomas and Keith Lambert at Worldwide Speakers Group in Alexandria, Virginia; Rich Gibbons, Jeff Bigelow, and Tim Mathy of Speak Inc. in San Diego, California; Brian Lord, Premiere Speaker Bureau in Franklin, Tennessee; Barrett Cordero of Big Speak in Santa Barbara, California; Julie Efaw of Capitol City Speakers Bureau in Springfield, Illinois; Jay Klahn of Dynamic Speakers in Dallas, Texas; Meghan Pritchard of the Lavin Agency in New York City and Toronto, Canada; Martin Perelmuter and Sundance Filardi of Speakers Spotlight in Toronto, Canada; Ed Adler of SME Entertainment Group in Los Angeles, California; James Robinson of Robinson Speakers Bureau in New York

City; Alex Alton with Creative Artists Agency in New York City; Angela Schelp of Executive Speakers Bureau in Memphis, Tennessee; Jo Borello of Eagles Talent in South Orange, New Jersey; Darrin Powell with Promentum Speakers of Dallas, Texas; Michael Steele of Greater Talent in New York City; Tamsen Browne Reed of Celebrity Speakers in Dallas, Texas; and Prakash Idnani, who represents me in India. They are all exceptional professionals.

My family life is private but I'm a married guy and we've been together since we were twenty-one years old, which means we're about to celebrate our thirty-eighth anniversary. That's a long time and life only gets better. Without the support and encouragement of my family, there's no way the time away from home for the research I do, the books I write, and the teaching and speeches I deliver could happen, and I wouldn't be able to say that between what I do for a living and my family I'm probably the happiest and most content man in the world.

Here's hoping this book exceeded your expectations. Please feel free to reach out to me at jason@jason-jennings.com.

By George, we got another one done!

Index

Index

Index

Index

Index

Index

Index